David,
Thanks for all you do
to strengthen men!
~Jack

The 7 Pillars of a
Legacy Minded Man

by

Joe Pellegrino
&
Jack Redmond

Jack Redmond

Prov. 27:17

1 cor 16:13-14

The 7 Pillars of a Legacy Minded Man
© 2014 Joe Pellegrino and Jack Redmond

ISBN: 978-1497373198

Edited by Susan Moeller

Printed in the United States of America
Legacy Minded Men ™

We would like to dedicate this book to our families who love us, our friends who support us and our Lord who saved us!

-Joe and Jack

Table of Contents

The 7 Pillars of a Legacy Minded Man

Pillar 1: Prayer

Prayer is the foundation of a lasting legacy. Through prayer, God opens our eyes to His will and plans, and He gives us the wisdom and power to live purposefully and build our legacy.

Pillar 2: Persona

Persona is who we are at our core. It is our true character and attitude toward life and people. Our legacy is the reproduction of our persona, and it is greatly shaped by our inner circle.

Pillar 3: Purity

Purity, especially sexual purity, is one of the MOST important things in a man's life. A man's thoughts and actions in this area have the power to bring clarity and focus or the power to ruin and distort EVERY other area of life.

Pillar 4: Purpose

Understanding purpose is the key to living out our destiny. Knowing and having purpose is the beginning point and driving force of building our legacy.

Pillar 5: Priorities

Life hands us an endless to do list that will eat away at all of our time and resources if we let it. Establishing and maintaining priorities allows us to develop a winning plan of attack!

Pillar 6: Perseverance

Tough times introduce a man to himself. Facing fear and trials will teach us not to quit, ever! While we are living our purpose and executing our game plan, we will have to go through tough times, be prepared!

Pillar 7: Power

When we chose to follow Christ, God filled us with the Holy Spirit. He brings the same power that raised Jesus Christ from the dead and into our lives and works through us! When the Holy Spirit is unleashed in our lives, He will provide new opportunities and the power to succeed!

Prologue

My name is Joe Pellegrino, and I am just a regular guy, an average Joe.

May 26, 1995 is my reset date. That day, during a Promise Keepers conference in Washington D.C., God offered me a "do-over," and I took it, putting my life in the hands of Jesus Christ. I realized what a shameful excuse of a man I had been for the first thirty-three years of my life -- so much sin. So much sin! But that all began to change the day I chose to walk with Jesus. Since then, my life has been a process of growth, transformation and at times failing forward.

Before I met Christ, I had been building my life like a man building his house on sand. My life lacked a solid foundation. That day in 1995, I traded the foundation of sand and replaced it with a life-foundation of solid rock! (see Luke 6:46-49) This new start gave me a strong base upon which to build my life, but that was only the beginning. I finally had the right foundation, but I still needed the rest of the house!

The internal structure, made up of pillars and beams, comes next and supports EVERYTHING else. Too many men stop with the foundation of their new life in Christ. But Jesus Christ didn't come just to save us from our sin. He came so that we could, through His power, build a new and different life.

Just as my life before Christ lacked a solid foundation, it also had faulty, shaky pillars. A pillar is for support, and several are required to hold up a structure. Up until that fateful day in D.C., my pillars either didn't exist or had crumbled under the weight of my life and my sin. My pillars were built with cheap, inferior materials. I was cutting corners, taking the easy way out in order to build my empire quickly, only to find my handiwork insufficient amidst the storms of life and beneath my personal weight of sin.

Through many painful life experiences, I learned that I would need something stronger and more reliable than myself as a foundation to build upon, and I learned that I would need better pillars to hold things up.

On that day in 1995, after thirty-three years of paying dearly for my faulty design, I began working from a better blueprint. I traded my life plans for God's. It was an awesome moment. And the journey of rebuilding a life began.

This book will point you toward the foundation of Jesus Christ and help you build a life on

Him. It will also point you to the kinds of structure Jesus wants for your life. The foundation and pillars we describe will result in a life of lasting impact. They are the keys to becoming a *Legacy Minded Man*.

As the founder of *Legacy Minded Men*, an organization dedicated to "engage, encourage & equip men to be who God created them to be," I've learned that when I take the time, make the right investment in materials, and have the right builder, it makes all the difference. I've discovered **7 Pillars** that can stand the test of life!

These **7 Pillars** are non-negotiable skills. Men can and should master them and use them to build a life. These pillars will hold up, no matter what your life looks like. And, they will outlast you.

You don't want to just have a good season or a good run. You want to have a good life. Your life will affect the generations that follow you. That is your legacy. If you build well, what you build will stand long after you leave this world.

This is the way a *Legacy Minded Man* thinks.

So what is "Legacy"?

leg·a·cy [**leg**-*uh*-see]
***noun, plural* leg·a·cies.**
1. *Law.* a gift of property, especially personal property, as money, by <u>will</u>; a bequest.
2. anything handed down from the past, as from an ancestor or predecessor

Source: dictionary.reference.com

A legacy is a gift of property, usually from an ancestor or predecessor. But, the definition could also include the skills and examples we learn from those who have gone before us.

A ***Legacy Minded Man*** lives so that he will have something valuable to hand down to his children, the next generation, the church and society as a whole. Some of these gifts are material, but many of the gifts we are interested in are spiritual or character-based.

The reality is that we all hand down something. Some people leave treasured gifts, others leave debt. Some leave great morals and family history; others leave utter chaos. Some leave a strong spiritual heritage; others leave generational sin. Chances are, you have certain possessions or character traits you are proud to hand down. Chances are even better that you have things you pray will end with you.

You're just like me. Before God began His work in my life, my legacy wasn't looking so good, so I made some changes. I believe you are man enough to make changes, too. If the legacy you are leaving now stinks, don't give up!

Yesterday is Gone, But You can Make Great Choices Today!

I've failed many times in my life. I've also had many successes. Both extremes have been part of my life. "The thrill of victory and the agony of defeat", I have lived through both.

While victory and success have driven me forward to do greater things, I've probably learned more from failure. That's because long ago, I decided to let failure be my life coach, inviting it to teach me what I REALLY needed to know.

Along the way, I decided that I would win in life. I also decided to live a life that would make a difference long after I was gone. I didn't want to be someone who lived comfortably now, but did nothing to make the world a better place. I also decided to help other men succeed where I had failed, and to teach them to be husbands and fathers in ways that I wasn't taught.

I want to invite you to choose victory in life and to choose to help others win. I would love to help you do this.

A *Legacy Minded Man* lives so that he wins, day in and day out. He honors God; he loves his wife; he trains his children; and he overcomes failure because he understands that God created him to succeed in life.

All of this is a process, and **The 7 Pillars of a Legacy Minded Man** is a map for the journey. You may swing and miss, but you get back to the plate and swing again. If you strike out, you work; you practice; you get coached; and then you step to the plate again. You keep at it. Then, when you're up in the bottom of the 9th, you hit that walk off home run. That's what God has created you to do. *Legacy Minded Men* is here to help you get there.

I am living proof that anyone can change! As a child, teen and young adult, I was a chronic liar. I lied so much that I believed the lies. To this day, I still cannot identify some events as the product of my imagination or real events that truly happened. I also accepted lies that society and the devil told me. Eventually, I learned from God's Word that the truth would set me free. I made the choice to stop the habitual lying, stop accepting the lies of others, and most importantly to stop living lies.

I also have known incredible success and excruciating failure. I raised $1.3 million dollars for a business that was personally endorsed by one of my sports heroes. Success! But things went very wrong, and the business went bankrupt. I ended up unemployed and in debt. Failure!

The belly up business venture was one of the most painful moments of my life. Through it, though, I met myself. God turned it all around with a lot of support from my wife and friends and a lot of hard work.

My prayer is that through **The 7 Pillars of a Legacy Minded Man,** God will help you win in life.

The **7 Pillars** will focus on God's Word – what does He say about life and how it should be lived? We'll answer questions like:

- *Why are the 7 **Pillars** crucial to building MY legacy?*
- *What does this look like in REAL life?*
- *How do I walk this out?*
- *How do I build these pillars in my life?*

Stories and examples listed in the **7 Pillars** are from me. If you see (Jack) then the story is being told by my friend and co-author Jack Redmond.

As you read this book you will find over 700 instances where the word "I" is used. Stanford University did a study that revealed that only 5 percent of their students were able to remember points made in a lecture when statistics were the foundation of the talk. But over 60 percent of the students were able to recall a lecture when an "I" story was introduced to cement the message. Therefore we felt led to share stories, primarily from our lives, to illustrate each **Pillar** presented. Some will make us look very bad. We're ok with that, because we know that we have all done things that we are ashamed of. Some will make us look good, but we're not trying to brag. We want to help you remember the pillars.

I've discovered it's easier to build a great legacy when you are surrounded by other *Legacy*

Minded Men. Join us. Our team is big and strong and growing EVERY day!

Like me you may be just an average Joe, imperfect in so many ways, but that should not stop us from being bold, and doing great things...in His name and for His glory. That's how I have chosen to live, what about you?

- *Joe Pellegrino, 4/2014*

Pillar 1:
Prayer - It All Starts Here

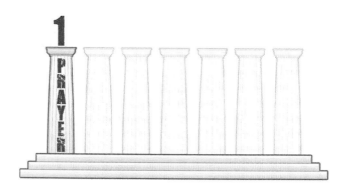

To be a Christian without prayer is no more possible than to be alive without breathing.
- Martin Luther

You desire but do not have, so you kill. You covet but you cannot get what you want, so you quarrel and fight. You do not have because you do not ask God.
- James 4:2

Are You REALLY Serious About Building a Legacy?

Caution: *This is the most important chapter in the book. It may scare you away! If you struggle to make* *prayer a significant part of your life, you aren't alone. Most men doubt the power of prayer, or they are bored by the thought of sitting still, talking to someone they can't see. A lot of you might be tempted to stop reading now because you aren't interested in praying longer or harder. Don't let the challenges keep you from reading on. This chapter can change your life. You're a man, if something is important to you, you will do it. If you're serious about building a legacy, you MUST be serious about being a man of prayer!*

Legacy Minded Men Choose Prayer

A ***Legacy Minded Man*** must be a man of prayer! Only through prayer can we discover, experience and achieve God's purposes. Only through prayer can we leave a solid physical legacy for the people we care about. And, only through prayer can we create a spiritual legacy that will bless our families' for generations to come. Prayer is one of the most important things that we can do!

But, from years of experience in ministry, we can tell you that prayer is not something men do naturally. It's often not their go-to play when the chips are down or their go-to when life is good, either.

* * * *

I (Jack) have talked to a lot of people who are mad at God. They have a problem or situation that they want God to change, and He hasn't done what they want. They rant and rave about the situation, and they blame God for not helping them. The funny thing is that when I ask them if they have prayed about their problem, often these same people look at me with a dumbfounded expression and say, "no."

* * * *

Most people want things and will go to extreme measures to get them. They quarrel, fight and even kill, as the Bible says, but they never take the time to pray and ask God for help.

We have two choices: Face our problems with our own strength and ability, or turn to God in prayer, so that we can face our problems with His strength and ability.

Legacy Minded Men Learn to Pray

Choosing to look for God's strength in prayer is just the first step. We have to learn some important lessons to be men of prayer – we have to learn to invest effort in something that doesn't come naturally to us, and we have to learn humility.

In general, as men, we are doers, not talkers, and the simplest definition of prayer is talking to God. God has wired us to get things done, and we resist sitting around running our mouths when we could be doing something "productive." To pray, we must learn how to spend time talking to God.

As men, we also like to be in charge — we want to fix things; we want to win. But prayer takes us out of the driver's seat. Prayer requires us to admit that we need God's help. That's humbling. Most people I know resist humility. But, in God's eyes, it's not optional. We must learn humility.

God's Grace and Power are released through Humility

But he gives us more grace. That is why scripture says: "God opposes the proud, but gives grace to the humble." - James 4:6

A great definition of grace is *God's empowering strength for us to do what He called us to do and be what He called us to be.* The Bible is clear. If we want that kind of strength, we've got to get over ourselves, and be humble.

So what is humility? The Bible gives a straight answer: "Do not think of yourself more highly than you ought, but rather think of yourself with sober judgment, in accordance with the faith God has distributed to each of you." Romans 12:3.

Humble people don't try to impress others or themselves by showing off. They see themselves clearly, as people whose best quality is their faith in God, and they shut up about the rest.

Isn't that countercultural to everything we are taught?

Humble? Missed that class.

Make-myself-look-good-at-all-costs? A+

The reality is that it takes more strength to be humble than it does to brag. Anybody can shoot his mouth off and act like he's the man! Anyone can be arrogant and try to do things solo. Bars across our nation are filled with guys who act like they are 10-feet tall and bulletproof while their marriages and lives stink!

It's harder to be humble and ask for God's help.

Be tough, suck it up, be a man: Be humble before God.

Kill It and Grill It?

Men who want to pray must learn to resist their natural inclination to act first and talk later. The desire to act is built into men by God, and it's valuable. But, that same wiring, apart from God's help, can keep us from being the men of prayer that God wants us to be. As men, we are at our best when we are being led by God, and not just by our urges and inclinations.

Those instincts run deep. Ever heard of the hunter-gatherer societies? Men were the hunters. The survival of a man's family depended to a large extent on his willingness and ability to get things done.

Our culture has mostly eliminated hunting for survival, but we would argue that accomplishing important tasks and achieving career goals are our modern day hunting.

Men want to see the prey, kill it, drag it home, and grill it. We don't want to sit around at a fancy restaurant talking about how the steak was prepared. We want to devour it!

By nature, we are doers. Unfortunately, prayer seems like a lot of sitting around. We want in on the action. Thankfully, God gives us the opportunity. Prayer is the key to kingdom action.

Real prayer is not passive. It is the way we aggressively take hold of what God has for us. It's the way we kill it and grill it in the Spirit. When we pray, we are in the ring, in the fight, bare-knuckled and bleeding. Praying is action, and it is where true victory is really won.

Without Prayer – We Will NEVER Be All That God Created Us to Be

The Bible is clear that God has a purpose for us. He made us to do "good works" that He prepared in advance for us (Eph. 2:10). Amazing, right? Choosing not to pray limits that purpose. Apart from God's power we are limited. In our own strength, we can NEVER do all that God created us to do! We must learn to become men of prayer if we will ever become men of legacy!

You can learn this the easy way, or you can learn it the hard way.

Unfortunately I chose the hard way.

If you really asked me what motivated me to become a man of prayer, the answer is simple – PAIN! Yup, you got it. In my failure – pain. In my inadequacy to change myself, people and situations – pain. When I looked into the mirror and didn't like what I saw – pain. When people that loved me criticized me (and I knew they were right) – pain. Many times I came to the end of myself and lost the game I was playing. I was forced to realize that without God's serious involvement in certain situations, I was going to lose and keep on losing. In prayer, I discovered that God could and would change me, and then use me to change the situation. My future victory could only be guaranteed if it was won in prayer.

Learning to Pray

If we truly want to be *Legacy Minded Men*, we must learn to be men of prayer. It's a challenge, but it's not impossible. It's also not a cookie-cutter skill. The way we relate to God in prayer looks different for different people.

Jack and I are no exception. A look at our prayer patterns might help you to create your own prayer style. Whatever works! Just do it.

Honestly I don't often have "prayer times" in the traditional sense of praying at set time periods, and I'm ok with that. For me, prayer is more of an ongoing conversation that I have with God. Here is what works for me:

Rejoice always, pray without ceasing, in everything give thanks; for this is the will of God in Christ Jesus for you. - 1 Thessalonians 5:16-18

My prayer life tends to follow this scripture. I try to live in a state of praise for all that God has already done for me, and He's done a lot! Throughout the day, I communicate to God, the Creator, that I am simply thankful for the new day, my job, my family, etc. I think that my willingness to praise God is a good test of my spiritual health. If I can't heap praise on the one who gave me life, then I need to conduct a strong examination of who I really am and what I really believe.

Thankfulness has helped me to keep my sanity through all of life's ups and downs. It reminds me of all that God has done, and how good He is! It makes me smile and places hope in my heart. It also keeps me from getting discouraged by all of the problems in the world.

In addition to praising and thanking God, I also ask Him for things throughout the day. There are always a million things running through my mind. I turn these thoughts into prayers. When a thought about a man I've been working with pops into my head, I turn his problem into a prayer. When I start to stress out about a bill I can't pay or a resource I don't have, I turn that concern into a prayer. I don't waste time worrying about what I don't have or haven't been able to do. Instead, I invite God into the situation and ask Him to take care of it!

When I meet people who are overwhelmed with their situations, I don't tell them I will pray for them LATER I do it then. Too many of us say we will pray for someone, but with all the distractions of life or a simple failure to care, we don't follow through. So I try to pray while the request is fresh. This honors God and the person who made the request. It's become my habit to constantly turn these problems and needs into prayers RIGHT at the time I am asked so that I do not forget!

Apart from praise and requests, I also like to just talk to God. He is my Father and is always there. He already knows everything that's going on and everything about me, so I don't have to hide. I come to Him, just as I am, and talk. People fail me, but He doesn't!

Another prayer habit I've developed is to keep a list of requests. As a business owner, husband, father etc. I have a lot of concerns, and a lot of requests.

At *Legacy Minded Men*, we spend our time and effort reaching out to men who have "man" issues. As I interact with these men, I learn about their needs and challenges, and my prayer list grows.

Over the years, I've learned to take care of my business and let God take care of His! So as I pray throughout the day, I continually trust that God hears and is working things out behind the scenes. This lifestyle of prayer has resulted in constant answered prayers! This has encouraged me to keep praying.

Prayer invites God into situations that seem hopeless to me and to the people involved in them. There are certain things that only God can truly change, and that's why I pray.

Prayer Works!

It was the summer of 2007, and my son Jordan, then 12 years old, was on his first mission trip. He went to Oswego, New York, to help rebuild a home. On one of the last days of the trip, he was working on the ground floor. His job was to pass 4 by

8 foot pieces of 5/8-inch plywood to the second floor. The workers on the second level would in turn pass the sheet to the top floor.

At the end of the day, Jordan and his team leader shoved a final sheet up. But when the crew on the second floor pushed it to the third level, no one was there to catch it. The third floor crew had mistakenly thought they were finished, and they weren't in place. Since there was nobody to grab it, the piece of 4-by-8 plummeted. Those who saw it yelled, "Run!" The team leader escaped, but my son tripped and the piece of plywood fell directly on his leg. The damage was significant. His leg was crushed, and his foot was actually dangling by the ligaments.

We got a call about the accident while Jordan was on his way to the hospital. When we asked what the damage was, they said it was most likely just a broken or fractured leg. They told us not to worry.

My wife got in our van and said, "I'm driving!" Then she drove like a bat out of hell to get to the hospital. On the way, we got a call from the doctor at the hospital who told us that Jordan needed surgery right away to remove pressure on his leg. The operation was done while we were still en route. They simply could not wait for us to get there because they feared that the bone was going to break through the skin if it continued to swell.

Fractured leg? Yeah...I don't think so!

By the time we arrived at the Oswego hospital, Jordan was out of the operating room, lying groggily in a hospital bed.

Unfortunately, because of the swelling, they couldn't put anything on his leg in terms of a cast. He was in a tremendous amount of pain, so we stayed in the hospital with him that night. The next day, we drove him to our local hospital where he could see a pediatric specialist. Because Jordan's leg didn't have any protection, he felt every bump we hit on the ride there.

The specialist gave us bad news: Jordan may never walk again. To make matters worse, he told us that the piece of plywood had gone through the middle of Jordan's growth plate, which probably meant that the leg would stop growing. It also meant that in order to keep both legs the same length, they would have to break Jordan's other leg, limiting its growth as well.

We refused to believe this report and turned to the Creator in fervent prayer (James 5:16). We prayed hard, and we told the doctor that, regardless of the prognosis, Jordan was going to be made whole again!

This boy had been significantly covered by prayer since before he was born, and we chose to continue to put his life, and his body, into the hands of the God we had learned to trust.

Later that year, when the cast finally came off, Jordan walked.

Can you say "Thank you Jesus!"

The doctors were amazed!

What's even more amazing is that Jordan played ball that next spring. He was able to pitch, hit and run the bases. Unbelievable! And, he has grown almost a foot since the doctors told us that his growth plates were too damaged to allow him to get any taller. As I write this, he is six feet one inch, the tallest member of our family. How could this have happened? Jordan's recovery defied the doctors. They could not understand how it happened. The answer is simple - prayer is powerful and it works!

* * * *

* * * *

Jack's 2 Cents on Prayer

For the first 10 years or so of my Christian walk, I wasn't consistently passionate about prayer. I did pray, and God answered many of my prayers. But, in reality, I was failing the humble test. I was thoroughly engrossed in pride.

Instead of evaluating myself based on the faith God gave me, like God tells us to do in Romans 12:3, I was comparing myself to other people. I concluded that I prayed as much or more than many of the people I knew, so I felt pretty good about myself. I was absolutely "thinking more highly of myself" than I should have.

Comparing ourselves to others is a dangerous game. Because I was "doing some things better" than the people I knew, I was satisfied. I didn't really think that I needed to focus on growing in my prayer life. Then, I met some powerful men and women of prayer. When I compared myself to them, I realized I was like an all-star on a junior high basketball team-- not a starter in the NBA!

* * * *

Prayer as Relationship

As we described earlier, men like to get things done, and I'm no exception. At times, I have seen prayer as the turbo-boost button my life. When I want to get big things done I need a big boost so I pray a big prayer. It's amazing to see God answer those big prayers.

I would be passionate about a situation and pray until it was "fixed" but after that, I was done. At times, I wanted God's power more than I wanted Him!

The pastor of my church challenged me to ask myself an important question: Am I a man who prays or a man of prayer? When I first heard the question, my inadequate prayer life was screaming at me! Yes, I prayed but I could not call myself a "man of prayer!"

Since hearing that question, I've been growing in this area. I've had to learn that certain things only happen with time, and certain things require lots of time if you want a deep and rich experience. I have learned to make prayer a greater priority, instead of making my works for Jesus *the* priority.

Set the Clock for Prayer, Schedule the Days

My prayer life hinges on two things. Like Joe, I love to pray throughout the day as different things are thrown at me. But I also build times for focused prayer into my daily schedule.

If I am going to spend significant times in prayer, I have to schedule them. What do I mean by that? First, I try to pray for 30 minutes each morning. I get up, go to my kitchen, put 30 minutes on the timer, and pray until it beeps. Some days I get distracted and skip, but for the most part, this is my morning routine. I also schedule days of prayer and fasting throughout the year. This may seem rigid, but it's what I have to do. Otherwise I will work, work, work and barely pray!

Like any new skill, at first it was tough to pray for 30 minutes, but over time, it's gotten easier. Many days now, the 30 minutes fly by, and sometimes, the 30 minutes doesn't seem long enough. There are times that I just keep going until I feel done.

To grow, I had to challenge myself. I had to stop accepting the status quo of my spiritual life. I realized my priorities were not lined up if I could watch a 2-3 hour game on TV and not spend 30 minutes with my Lord and Savior. I'm not saying

there is anything wrong with watching a ball game –
invite me over, let's eat some hot wings! But, mature
faith and spiritual legacy don't happen by watching a
football player make a tackle or score a touchdown!

Seasons of Prayer and Fasting

As a new Christian, I was so excited about all
that God was doing in my life, I wanted more. Every
time I did something my pastor or other leaders in the
church told me to do, it was like my spiritual life was
turbo-boosted to the next level!

So, in 1998, when my pastor declared that the
church was going on a 10-day fast, I was in.

It was a partial fast. You could eat one meal a
day but skip the other two. The idea was that in
addition to your regular prayer time, you would use
the time you normally spent on those missed meals to
pray instead.

I went for it -- no breakfast, no lunch. I read
my Bible and prayed instead. The solution to
problems I was facing in life became much clearer,
and I felt God more. Over the years, I have continued
to fast periodically, sometimes just skipping two
meals, other times foregoing everything but water. I
can honestly say that every time I have fasted, I have

experienced growth, greater clarity and increased closeness and leading of the Lord.

Fasting has been especially helpful when I needed spiritual renewal or help in breaking down Satan's strongholds like lust, anger or unforgiveness. Fasting weakens and pushes the flesh down while strengthening your spirit. This allows you to overcome the flesh, be healed, and become more like Jesus!

Legacy Minded Men Are Men of Prayer!

Legacy Minded Men don't stay stuck in discouragement: they turn their problems into prayers and watch God turn their situations around!

Prayer is work! One reason that men avoid it is because they perceive prayer as passive. But, when men deliberately engage in times of prayer, they find out that its hard work, and many of them give up! Becoming a man of prayer will not happen by accident. It takes training — just like an athlete working on a physical challenge; prayer is a spiritual challenge that takes effort. It's worth it. The recipe for spiritual victory ALWAYS includes prayer!

As men, we face a constant flow of demands, problems and crisis situations. We have a choice. We can tackle these problems in our own strength, or we can pray for God's help! Just like a runner or football player eating plates of pasta before the competition, prayer is our fuel to keep going.

By establishing the pillar of prayer, you can bring God into every situation you pray about. On your own, you are limited. Prayer invites God's constant presence and infinite power to bear on your problems. Prayer is also a key part of building the other pillars of your legacy.

Just a Thought...

Is there someone in your life that you really want to learn from? If you could meet with that person every day, for as long as you like, would you do it? Of course you would. You can spend WHATEVER time you wish with the Creator of the universe. The question is why don't you?

Pillar Builders...

- Be ready to pray – all the time
- Have a list of prayer items
- Constantly thank God for what He is doing
- Set a deliberate time of prayer each day
- Establish times of prayer that include fasting throughout the year

Additional Study Verses...

2 Chron 7:14, Jer 33:3, Jer 29:11-13, Matt 5:44, Matt 6:9, Mark 11:24. 1 Thess 5:16-18, James 4:2, James 4:6, James 5:16, Rev 5:8

Pillar 2:
Persona - Who You Are...
Is Who You Are!

Be yourself: everyone else is already taken.
— Oscar Wilde

The position a person occupies in the world depends on the quantity and the quality of the service he renders plus the mental attitude which he relates to others.
— Andrew Carnegie

Hello World, This is Who I Am

Your persona, or personality, is how you portray yourself to others. Persona is a combination of your gifts and talents, preferences, thoughts and attitudes. It determines your tendency to act in a certain way in any given situation.

You can think of persona as your default way of interacting with the world. Are you loud? Quiet? Helpful? Irritable? Do you act like a grumpy old man or a rich young ruler? Are you more of a leader or more of a follower?

Some people use their persona to hide who they really are. There is little consistency between their inner and outer lives: their personality is a mask.

Casinos in Las Vegas have mastered the trick. One with an Eiffel Tower pretends to be Paris; another with a Statue of Liberty masquerades as New York; and a casino built like a massive pyramid imitates Egypt. They're all facades. Visitors, no matter how much they want to believe otherwise, are still playing slots in the middle of the Nevada desert.

A man of integrity with a healthy persona doesn't wear a mask. His persona portrays who he really is, all the time, no matter what the situation.

Ideally, our personalities honor God and bless others. Sometimes, they don't.

Our personalities have been shaped by our

surroundings and experience, our upbringing, our trials and struggles, our victories and failures. Results may vary!

There is good news and bad news about persona. The bad news is that by the time we are adults, some parts of our personalities are pretty much set. But, with the right input, a lot of the aspects of our personas can be shaped and changed.

Will the Right Persona Please Stand Up?

Many men are confused about who they are supposed to be. The ideal male persona has been the subject of a lot of debate. On one hand, men are told to be strong providers who never waiver. Then, in the next breath, they are told to be soft and sensitive. They are bombarded with contradictory demands that no one person could ever hope to live up to.

In an ideal world, every boy and young man would be surrounded with caring adult role models who could point the way to the right persona. Sadly, we are living in a far from ideal world, and many men flounder in a jumbled mess of mixed messages about manhood.

Lacking role models and teachers, even men who accurately determine their target persona still struggle to create it. They are often expected to know things and act in ways they haven't been taught.

This is where God makes all the difference. He purposely created and gifted you to be YOU! Your strength is in THAT, not in some manufactured personality that someone else wants you to adopt. Jumping through hoops to make people happy may work temporarily, but it is no way to live life.

We are shaped, good or bad, by our upbringing, and we are at our best when we have a strong character and a great attitude. But there is a sweet spot in how God wired us. As *Legacy Minded Men,* we need to live out the persona God intended us to have.

Persona Improvement Plan

Attitude and character are two critical aspects of our persona. Luckily for us, both of these respond well to training.

Attitude, according to the dictionary, consists of the feeling, disposition or orientation of mind we have toward a person or thing. The classic example is of two people who both look at a glass of water. One person smiles and declares the glass half full. The other frowns and declares it half empty. The tendency to see the glass as full or empty is attitude.

One of the best ways to begin working on your attitude is to notice it. A lot of times, people just feel how they feel. They don't really ask themselves if a different mindset is possible or desirable. As believers in Jesus, we have a lot of reasons to have a good attitude. God has promised to be with us always; He has given us His Spirit to live inside of us; He has given us power over our sinful tendencies; and He loves us unconditionally. Armed with those truths, men can face their present situation and their fears for the future with a sense of hope. They can, as the saying goes, "Stay calm and carry on." That's the kind of attitude that characterizes a *Legacy Minded Man*.

The other indispensable aspect of persona is character. According to the dictionary, character has three aspects. First, it's the sum of all the parts that add up to who we are. Second, it's our moral or ethical behavior, and finally, it is our reputation.

J. Oswald Sanders, in his classic book "Spiritual Leadership," underlines the importance of character. He wrote, "Every Christian is under obligation to be the best he can be for God." As *Legacy Minded Men*, we need to take character development seriously.

If you want to have the best possible character, you have to get serious about how you act around other people. Are you likeable, friendly, and positive? Or, are you difficult to talk with, hard to get to know, or whiny? If you fall into the second group, it's time to change. No matter how entrenched these behaviors are, you can do better.

Being serious about character also requires a zero-tolerance policy when it comes to bad morals or ethics. Not many of us will attend military school, but the cadet honor code at West Point can guide us ethically. It says, "Don't lie, cheat, steal or tolerate those who do."

Finally, think about your reputation. Do people trust you? Should they? If your mistakes in the past have left you with a bad reputation, it's time to start building a new one. Go to the people you have hurt and ask for their forgiveness. Tell them you are sorry. But, don't stop there. You must rebuild trust by showing people that you are trustworthy. Start small. Be on time for work; take out the trash when you are supposed to; pay your bills.

While it's certainly possible, and many times desirable, to work on our personas, it's not easy. We need the help of our friends.

Inner Circle – Spouse, Family, Close Friends, Business Partners

Many men are distant from their spouses and have few, if any, close friends. They lack the right people in their lives to help them achieve spiritual, business or financial success. These men suffer from "Lone Wolf" syndrome. They are Lone Rangers without Tonto; Tarzan without Jane; George Steinbrenner without the Yankees!

People survive like this, but they don't flourish. God did not create us to be lonely, unsupported, or disconnected from others. Your inner circle has a HUGE impact on the quality of your life – your emotions, your fulfillment, your spiritual walk, and your financial status.

Friends can make or break your persona. The negative impact of friends is spelled out in 1 Corinthians 15:33. It says, "*Bad company corrupts good character.*" I believe that the reverse is also true: Good company corrupts bad character just as powerfully. Friends will push you to be better or help you to be worse. Who you choose matters.

John Maxwell, in his book "The 21 Irrefutable Laws of Leadership," says, "Every leader's potential is determined by the people closest to him." I not only agree with Maxwell, I would expand that law to include every *Legacy Minded Man*.

Understanding the Power of Inner Circle

I understand the Lone Ranger way of thinking. I grew up as a loner. I was a loner as a businessman, and I didn't have any close, confiding relationships until much later in life.

Until *Legacy Minded Men* became reality I did not realize the negative impact of my Lone Wolf status. For the first time I truly realized that I needed to be part of a team. I was ready to surround myself with solid men.

Because of my past, it was a bumpy process. Until *Legacy Minded Men* began, most of the people who said they "cared" about me usually only did so because they wanted something from me. As a result of those experiences, I struggled to differentiate between people who were playing me and people who truly cared.

Over time, the Lord has made it easier for me. Here's the test I use: The people who truly care about you keep coming back and asking how you are doing, no matter your personal circumstances.

One such person is my good friend Jim Henry. When I was recruiting men to be part of what would become **Legacy Minded Men,** a friend of mine suggested I contact Jim. We met shortly after that, and I poured the vision out to him. The whole time, he listened but did not react at all. Because I'm an emotional Italian, I took his silence as a sign that he was disinterested. But when I finished, he finally spoke. To my surprise, he said two simple words, "I'm in." I was ecstatic! Since then Jim has become a second father to me, a man for whom I will do anything. My inner circle was being built.

Your Dad – Key to Your Inner Circle

Train a child in the way he should go, and when he is old, he will not turn from it. - Proverbs 22:6 (KJV)

Fathers Have a Huge Impact on how Their Sons Live as Adult Men

Your relationship with your dad sets the "norms" for you. God's purpose for fathers is to establish norms, boundaries and behaviors that are godly and wise. According to Proverbs 22:6, they are supposed to train their children, showing their children how to navigate through life.

Many men have benefited from the influence of great fathers.

But others have been left floundering because they didn't have a dad who taught them how to live as a man. Sadly, the number of men who grew up without the influence and teaching of an involved father is growing.

According to the U.S. Department of Justice, "Fatherlessness is a growing problem in America, one that undergirds many of the challenges that families are facing. When dads aren't around, young people are more likely to drop out of school, use drugs, be involved in the criminal justice system, and become young parents themselves."

Obviously, more men than ever are left scrambling to survive without the valuable training a good dad gives. These men don't have game plans, or the plans they have are faulty. When life's storms hit, these fatherless men don't have a plan, and the most important member of their inner circle —dear old dad—isn't there to lean on.

Persona in Action: A Case Study

Mike Tyson said, "Everybody has a plan until they get hit!" He was an incredibly gifted fighter with a super work ethic. But, that wasn't enough to succeed in life. When he was in a tough situation, his persona fell short. A closer look at his life story shows how the key ingredients for a great persona were not in place for Tyson.

In an autobiographical piece he wrote for New York magazine, Tyson describes his growing up years. According to Tyson, his dad wasn't around, and his mother was drunk "all the time." After getting beaten up at school, Tyson quit going – he was seven. Soon afterward, he got involved with a gang and began robbing homes. Then at the urging of other kids, he took up fighting, earning both money and respect. He was arrested often. At 12, Tyson was sent away to a juvenile detention center.

As a child and young teen, Tyson's inner circle was rotten to the core, but it was all he had. "Some people might read some of the things I'm talking about and judge me as an adult, call me a criminal," Tyson wrote. "But I did these things over 35 years ago. I was a little kid looking for love and acceptance, and the streets were where I found it. It was the only education I had, and these guys were my teachers" Tyson wrote.

At the juvenille detention center, Tyson met Cus D'Amato, a boxing trainer who would change his life. D'Amato promised to make Tyson "the youngest heavyweight champion of all time." Tyson recalls that comment from D'Amato as the first time he ever heard anyone say something nice about him.

Tyson's inner circle now included D'Amato. The older man definitely helped Tyson win, but the influence was geared toward boxing. "Cus wanted the meanest fighter that God ever created," Tyson wrote. "He trained me to be totally ferocious, in the ring and out."

When D'Amato passed away, Tyson was left floundering. Divorces and bankruptcy, a rape conviction and prison followed. Like so many other men, Tyson didn't have a father to teach him life skills. He failed often, publicly, and damagingly. While he was alive, Cus had protected Tyson, but he hadn't left him the kind of legacy Tyson could rely on. Let's take a look at how his lack of inner circle in his private life led to the downfall of his career.

Perhaps the most graphic illustration of the character weakness Tyson struggled with occurred during the 1997 World Boxing Association Championship fight with Evander Holyfield. Tyson was in a tight spot, and he responded like the "meanest...totally ferocious" fighter that D'Amato had trained him to be – he bit off the top of

Holyfield's ear. His boxing license was temporarily suspended and he was disqualified from the match.

Trading a Bad Persona for a Worse One!

We can all criticize Tyson and other celebrities for their lack of persona or their bad persona. But, the reality is that it took me a couple of tries at it before I got it right. You may be in the same boat.

Growing up, I was an awkward kid with a lot of pimples. As I've said, I was often a loner. I had friends, but no close relationships. I liked girls but wasn't exactly the most popular guy with the ladies. I had pretty low self-esteem.

All of this led to a conclusion: I would give myself a personality makeover while I was in college. No one at my school had known me before, so I saw the start of my career in college as an opportunity for a personality do-over. I decided to reinvent myself.

What new persona did I choose? The big mouth guy who showed off at every opportunity. I was convinced that some girls would like it, and I thought that this particular persona would earn me respect from other guys. It worked!

A couple of positives came out of my improvement experiment. I learned that it was possible to change my persona and with it, other people's perceptions of me. I also learned that I was more of a leader than I knew.

But, the new me had a dark side. I basically became really good at being a shallow jerk. The new persona was simply a façade to mask my insecurity – it didn't solve the problem. It just kept it out of sight.

The result of all my effort to change my persona amounted to a temporary fix for an immature kid. Instead of having character, I became a character!

My Big Mouth Helped Me NOT Get a Job!

It took me awhile to figure out that the "new and improved" Joe wasn't a winning persona. When I was around 23, I was a hotshot staff accountant at the Witco Chemical Corporation. My aura at the time was that my poop didn't stink. Other people's might, but not mine.

I decided to venture out and look for a new job. A headhunter set up an interview for me in a nearby town. I don't remember the name of the company, but I sure remember the meeting.

My interviewer was a young guy who immediately made me feel very confident and very comfortable. About half way through the interview, I planted my feet firmly on his desk. We talked about women, partying and all of my considerable conquests. When I left, he gave me a slap on the back and told me he looked forward to seeing me soon.

I left feeling absolutely positive that I had gotten the job. When I arrived home, there was already a message on my machine. The call was from my headhunter.

Her first message was this, "Joe, I just heard from the company and unfortunately, you did not get the job." When I heard those words, my heart sank. The rejection didn't make sense to me. I thought I had connected with the interviewer on a spiritual level.

But the next words that came out of her mouth changed the way I looked at myself. She said, "Oh, by the way, he has a message for you: 'Grow up'!"

I realized then that during the interview, the interviewer was testing me. He wanted to see how far I would go. He opened the door, and I just ran my mouth. What was impressive to a 23 year-old whose life was a mess was VERY unimpressive in the real world!

Based on my record, I should have qualified for the job. I had skills and a passion that seemed like a slam dunk for success.

What I lacked was a good persona. I was undisciplined, and my priorities were all out of whack. My carefully cultivated college persona let me down.

What I needed was another persona overhaul. But this time, I needed the help of an inner circle of people who would encourage me to develop a Godly attitude and character.

Until that time came, my persona was a liability.

When Life Hits Us

We said earlier that persona is our default way of interacting with the world around us. My default persona was on display when I felt comfortable in a job interview. But oftentimes our default persona is most clearly revealed in times of crisis. For Tyson, it was the fight with Holyfield, for others it's a loss, a financial struggle or a temptation.

Who are you in those moments? Do you default to anger or confusion, drinking or drugs, pornography or illicit sex?

Without an established character, a good attitude, and a strong inner circle, survival instinct will kick in, and you may find yourself doing stupid things to cope with the pain.

If you have the right inner circle and a strong personality, you will default to good character and positive attitude, dust yourself off and modify your game plan.

Tragedy and crisis hit all men. Your persona will either rise up to keep you going or crumble under the pressure. You WILL get hit. What is your plan?

Just a Thought...

You can't turn back the clock or erase the past. I shared some stories from my life that make me wish I could go back and have a do-over. But real life isn't like that. Not too many do-overs! Below are the three areas that make up YOUR persona. Like we said, you may not get do-overs in all areas, but God does give us new days to do things differently. If you could fast forward one year from today, what would these three areas look like, and what would you change about them?

Pillar Builders...

Attitude:

1) What needs to change?

2) What are you willing to do specifically to change in your attitude?

Character:

1) What is the biggest area of character that you need to change?

2) List at least 3 ways or actions you can take to build a stronger character:

Inner Circle:

1) Are you connected with and surrounded with the people you need to be a *Legacy Minded Man*?

2) What type of people do you need in your life to be everything God created you to be and do what God created you to do? Here are some areas where we need coaching and possibly different coaches based on the area:

- Spiritual
- Successful singleness
- Husband & Father
- Financial/Career

3) How can you find and include these people in your life?

4) Want to find out who you really are? Take a piece of paper and list your strengths on one side and your weaknesses on the other. Be completely honest. Then share your list with someone you love and trust. Ask them to review your list and provide you honest feedback. Just hold on tight, and if you hear something you don't like don't go nuts. Just listen and maybe you can learn something about yourself.

Additional Study Verses...

Pro 5:22, Pro 12:5, Pro 14:12, John 3:30, John 8:44,
John 14:6, 1 Cor 1:24:31, 1 Cor 15:33,
1 Cor 16:13-14, Phil 1:27

Pillar 3:
Purity – The Pathway to God's Presence and Power!

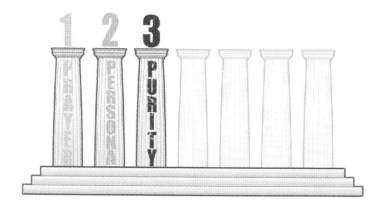

Most men usually have one of two weaknesses –
money or honey!
- Anonymous

The concept of "purity" isn't a big hit at most bars or ball games, and it doesn't come up a lot in boardrooms, either! But where God is concerned, purity means the difference between being connected or disconnected from Him! That connection matters because we are blessed and transformed in His Presence. Apart from that, we are on our own.

*Who may ascend the hill of the LORD? Who may
stand in his holy place? He who has clean hands and
a pure heart, who does not lift up his soul to an idol
or swear by what is false. He will receive blessing
from the LORD and vindication from God his Savior.*
- Psalm 24:3-5

A **Legacy Minded Man** takes personal purity
seriously. They have to -- It's the main area where
Satan attacks most men. Purity paves the way to
connecting with God, being in His Presence, knowing
Him. Sin and lack of purity do the opposite -- keeping
us from God's presence, love and power.

To put it simply, if you purposely live an
impure life, you will be on your own. You will have
chosen your sin instead of God. Your legacy, instead
of resembling the glory of God, will resemble you –
in all your impurity and brokenness.

In the past, when people used the phrases,
"You are a chip off the old block," or "You are just
like your father," it was a compliment. Now, because
our culture has become so impure and broken, when a
mother yells, "You are just like your father," it
typically follows some type of personal failure, and
it's often a slap in the face.

Hand or Heart Sanitizer, Anyone?

Clean hands and a pure heart are the recipe to connect with God on a regular basis. Clean hands represent the things we touch, the things we choose to do. Are our hands committed to our wives only, or are they the tools that search out internet pornography and cause us to dream of other women?

A pure heart represents what we love. Is our heart filled with affection for God and His people, or is it filled with greed for money? Do we trust God to provide, or are we cooking the books at tax time? Is our next car or next house more important than God? Do we cringe when the Pastor asks us to support the church or a missionary because it would mean sacrificing tickets to the next ball game? If our answer is yes, those things – the tax refund, the house, the car, the game -- have become idols. They are occupying our hearts and dirtying our hands.

In Exodus, the Bible tells us how God's people decided as a group to make an idol. They went to their leader and demanded that he make a golden calf for them to worship. In our day and age, we don't usually take a vote and petition Congress for something concrete to worship. But, we do let idols creep into our lives, making us unclean or impure. Over time, these misplaced loves and wrong actions pry us away from God.

The Benefits of a Pure Heart

Verse 5 of Psalm 24 tells us that God's concern for our purity is broader than simply stopping us from sin. He wants to bless us with joy. So often we think of God as an angry boss who is just looking for an opportunity to fire us. Instead, we need to see God as the ultimate coach. When good coaches tell a player what not to eat, or set a curfew, or requires wind sprints, it's because they want us to win. And, they want to celebrate the victory with us. God is like a good coach. He not only wants to save us from sin, but He wants to be a continual blessing in our lives. A clean heart and pure hands are the recipe to receive and fully enjoy that blessing!

Money or Honey – What's YOUR Poison?

Men are generally interested in 3 things: the Bedroom, the Ballgame and the Billfold.
- Anonymous

It has often been said that men have one of two weaknesses – money or honey! That's right – cash or women. Ball games are pretty innocent, so we'll just skip them for now. But money and honey, those can be much different stories. Usually one or the other is the downfall of men who fall. Let's be clear, God often provides you with both. If you are called to be married, God wants you to have a great wife and a solid relationship. And, God clearly tells believers in 1 Timothy 5, that they are to provide financially for their families. Proverbs is full of advice that can make a business grow or an employee succeed. But, in our spiritual battle, the enemy of your soul will always try to take what God has for us and twist it. He wants us to use good things for our destruction instead of God's blessing.

I am a businessman. I work hard to make money, and so should you. I am also married and enjoy the benefits of a physical relationship with my beautiful wife. But, as a believer, I have to guard myself against greed and lust. The world teaches us to wrongly pursue sex and money, and our flesh sometimes desires them, too. Ironically, if we indulge our flesh and obey the world, we are poised to lose the good blessings – loving wives and good jobs -- that God has provided.

Training From Our Dads

Personal purity is another place where our relationship with our father — or lack of relationship — has a huge impact.

In a perfect world, we would all grow up in a healthy family with two parents who are committed for life to each other and who demonstrate and teach us all the things that we need to know. The reality is often much different. Lacking that parental guidance, the world, the flesh and the devil start a tag team wrestling match that often lands us outside of God's boundaries, and leaves us with dirty hands and a stained heart.

Dad's Sex Talk

Unfortunately, like a lot of parents, my dad didn't give me a lot of advice about sex and relationships. But, when I went off to college, he decided to throw in his two cents. As I was getting ready to leave home, he delivered his entire, amazing version of sex education in two words. He said, "Be careful."

That was it: my dad's entire life's wisdom on teaching his son about sex – all two words of it! Telling an 18-year-old boy to be careful, then setting him loose at college with no rules, no morals and hundreds of women is like telling a hungry shark not to eat, then throwing bloody fish parts in front of him. It shames me to say that I did not even follow those two simple words...I wish I did!

One guy I know has taken teaching his sons about purity a lot more seriously than my dad did. He purchased a curriculum from a Christian bookstore that begins with teaching about body parts and goes from there, covering puberty and God's design for sex in marriage.

He handles the formal "sex talks" differently with each kid. One of his boys is a little more reserved, so my friend just gives him the material to read, then follows up with an opportunity to ask questions. There usually aren't any, and that particular kid, an early teen, appears to be totally embarrassed by the whole process. My friend isn't put off by that. He wants his son to have good information, and he wants to be the one to provide it. It's a legacy issue.

The other kid is more open, so my friend announces the next sex talk with a little more fanfare. They read through the books out loud together, with the kid adding helpful comments like, "No way!" and, "Are you kidding me?" With this kid, it's all my friend can do to hold it together and not laugh at his son's reaction. Again, it's a legacy issue.

In this family, these formal sessions with dad help to keep sexuality an open topic. A lot of times, if an adult brings up an issue, kids will perceive that the subject is safe to talk about.

The method used to pass down Biblical sexual values will vary a lot from family to family. But, the important thing is to make sure it happens. Very few kids are going to sit down with you at dinner and ask about your sex life! The responsibility for telling them what they need to know about God's plan for sex is on you -- their dad. If you just can't make yourself go there, consider delegating it to your wife, or enlist another trusted adult.

Believe me, if you don't teach them, life will, and it won't be a good education. Make Biblical teaching on sex available to your sons, and make your legacy a good one.

Yankee Chapel

Purity doesn't just have to do with sex; it also has to do with the motives of our hearts. I learned this in a very costly way. When I was a young Christian, just out of the gate, I was asked to speak to a group of 70-year-old men by Dave Swanson, the head of Baseball Chapel, an organization that brings church to minor and major league stadiums around the country.

I had been taught to pray before you speak, asking God for the words. Then, just let it rip. For me, the formula sounded like this: **Prayer + open mouth = impressive message**.

So, that's what I did. In his kindness, the Lord blessed me, and I sensed Him speaking clearly through me. There was not one "ah" or "um." It was an awesome time, and when it was over, many of the men came up to me, and said things like, "Young man, keep talking," or "Boy, did you encourage me." I went home pumped up.

The following day Swanson asked me to speak at the Sunday chapel service at Yankee Stadium prior to the scheduled game between the Yanks and the Baltimore Orioles.

I knew that speaking to a bunch of 70-year-old men was an entirely different ballgame than speaking to the New York Yankees. I had been having a lot of interaction with players as I researched my book **Safe at Home**, but this was different. This was speaking to these men on a spiritual level.

Dave didn't take no for an answer.

The next morning after breakfast, we jumped in the car and headed to Yankee Stadium. Swanson showed me to the room where I would speak. And, he let me know that there would be two sessions: one for the Yankees and one for the Orioles.

Following the same plan as my last talk, I went to the men's room and prayed to the Lord. "Take over just like the other day," I asked. "Speak through me." The Orioles came in and once again, it was awesome, everything just went perfect, no "ahs" or "ums" it was flawless. The guys slapped me on the back and said, "Well done." Again, I was pumped!

There were 15 minutes between the Orioles' chapel and the Yankees' chapel, but instead of going back into that men's room and praying, I did a walk around. I paced around in circles thinking, "Wow, I'm really good at this. This is something I'm really good at. I'm as good as my pastor! Maybe I can be the next Billy Graham!"

I fed myself all of this self-absorbed garbage, which was, in essence, evil talk.

Before I knew it, the door flew open and 17 Yankees walked in. I knew some of them, and I was happily thinking, "You guys can just get ready to get blessed!"

Dave introduced me. I had the floor.

I opened my mouth and nothing came out! I forgot everything I was going to say, and I started a "hummina, hummina, hummina" kind of thing.

For out of the abundance of the heart the mouth speaks.
- Matthew 12:34

Lacking anything else to present, I started telling the story of how Dave and I met. I guess at the time, I thought it was an important and spiritually edifying story. It might have been, but I also embellished it juuusssst a little bit! I stretched the truth so badly, that Dave interrupted me and said, "Now, that's not true." Major league "ouch!"

You belong to your father, the devil, and you want to carry out your father's desires. He was a murderer from the beginning, not holding to the truth, for there is no truth in him. When he lies, he speaks his native language, for he is a liar and the father of lies.
- John 8:44

Now, whenever I speak, I always tell people, if you want to be humbled, be called a liar publicly while doing chapel for the New York Yankees!

Joe's Purity Journey – From Liar to Legacy Minded Man

You see, what we say comes out of our hearts, so our words are a great test of the purity of our hearts. And, truthfulness is one of the first and best tests for the purity of our words.

When you lie, you are connecting yourself with the father of lies – the devil. When you tell the truth, you are connecting yourself with Jesus, who actually IS truth! Most people have never looked at it this way. Purity or impurity are also a lot like snowballs rolling down a hill. The longer they roll, the bigger they get. When we lie, we open the door for the devil to have power in our lives. Believe me that just makes the lying snowball more massive! On the other hand, telling the truth shuts out the devil and opens the door for Jesus and His power to come into our situations, creating one holy snowball of truth.

The Early Joe – I Was Working on a Ph.D. in Lying and Deception!

As I said earlier, when I was a kid, I told many lies because I wanted to be somebody, somebody I wasn't. When I was small, I was scrawny. I got beat up. I got taken advantage of. Anybody who has had those experiences knows they play in your head. They make you angry, and they cause you a lot of angst in social situations. When I was young I handled all of this by lying.

People lie because they want something they don't have, or they lie to avoid something that is painful. I wanted to be stronger than I was, and I wanted to avoid the pain of being weak and inferior to those around me. So I lied.

Another reason people lie is because it works – at least for the moment. Just like a house of cards, lies will stand up for a while and look good doing it. But, as soon as that first gust of wind hits, they topple.

That was my pattern early on. Build a house of lies and hope I wasn't around when it crumbled.

Remember, our legacy is our pattern. If our lifestyle is a mess, our legacy -- the lives of people who follow us -- will be too. We wake up one day to see our kids repeating or "improving" on our sins, making them worse than ever. In effect we teach our kids how to sin.

As *Legacy Minded Men*, we need to see our own purity as a priority so that we can help our kids to avoid sin by leaving them a legacy of pure living.

Teaching My Son to Lie

Early in my parenting life, I had a chance to see my lying transferred to my son. My wife and I took our small children to Hershey Park in Pennsylvania. Joey was three-years-old, and Jennifer was about a year. Our funds were low, so I paid attention to a sign that said kids two and younger didn't have to pay admission.

As we got close to the gate, I picked up my son and whispered in his little ear, "If they ask you how old you are, say you are two." I carried him to add to the illusion. Sure enough, he got in free. It was a great day at the park.

Remember how we said that in stressful situations we resort to our default persona? Standing in line at the park, I was stressed. I was wrestling with the shame that I didn't have a lot of money. As men, we often feel that money is power, and when we lack money, we feel powerless. When I felt like I didn't measure up financially, I went to my default persona – a frequent liar. Without even knowing it, I was building that kind of default legacy for Joey.

On the way home, we stopped on the New Jersey Turnpike for a burger. My son, who was incredibly cute and talkative, began chatting with the people in the next booth. The lady sitting there asked how old he was. I'll never forget his answer. "Well, I'm three years old, but when I go to Hershey Park, I'm two." Man did I feel like a worm!

There is a way that seems right to a man, but its end is the way of death. - Prov. 14:12

You see, telling my son to lie "seemed right" while I was in line. "It's only a little lie," was the popular phrase running through my head as was the reality that my wallet was light. In the end, the money I saved wasn't worth it. Something in me died when I realized that I had used my son and taught him to lie just to save a few dollars.

But my sin and my mistake taught me something, too. I had an impure character that needed to be disinfected by the gospel. There was a lying side of me that needed to be buried.

I had a choice. Would my legacy to Joey be the impure example of a habitual liar, or the pure example of a godly man who honored truth? The change had to begin in me. Thank God that He didn't give up on me that day. Even though I knew I needed to change, it wasn't until Jesus empowered me that I really changed.

I've learned that if God does something for someone else He can do it for me too. You can be confident that if He did it for me...He can also do it for you!

Just a Thought...

When I (Jack) moved into a new neighborhood, I quickly became friends with my beer drinking, constantly cussing neighbors. I was a little different. I quit cussing and drinking when Christ saved me in 1997! Behind my back, they started joking about me. Then they challenged each other not to curse. Someone broke out a coffee can, and they made a bet. Every time one of them cursed, they had to put a dollar in the can. That lasted for about a weekend until they stopped because they couldn't afford their habit! I would just laugh and remind them that without Jesus, they'd be stuck with their potty mouths forever. The coffee can proved it!

You may not struggle with lying or cussing, but there is probably some area of your life that requires some fine tuning at the least, or maybe even a total overhaul!

Here are a couple of questions to ask yourself to get the ball rolling in the right direction.

- What is it that you want to change when it comes to "purity?"
- What steps should I take to walk this out in my life?

Pillar Builders...

– Purity Protectors

One of the ways that you can maintain purity is to have certain things in place to protect you from impure thoughts and actions. One way to look at these are as "purity protectors." When we play football, we wear equipment to shield us from injury. In life, we have insurance to guard us and to help us when things get tough or go wrong. A *Legacy Minded Man* builds purity protectors into his life, and he teaches his sons to do the same thing.

1) Friends – who do you have in your life who REALLY knows you and can ask you REAL questions.

2) Accountability partner – this can be HUGE in helping you stay on track. This is a MUST if you have a history of pornography, drugs/ or alcohol abuse, or other ongoing issues. An accountability partner is someone who has your permission to know your personal actions and thoughts and to help you avoid impure actions. Here are 10 great questions for your partner to ask you and for you to ask him:

1. How are you doing with God?
2. How are you doing with your mate or the person you're dating?
3. How are you doing with your children?
4. What temptations are you facing and how are you dealing with them?
5. How has your thought life been this week?
6. Are you consistently living for Christ in your workplace?
7. Have you been spending regular time in the Word and in prayer?
8. With whom have you been sharing the gospel?
9. Have you lied in your answers to any of the questions above?
10. How may I pray for you and help you?

3) Wife – you should not have to hide things from your wife. For long-term intimacy, she needs to trust you, and you need to trust her.

Additional Study Verses...

Psa 24:3-5, Matt 5:8, Matt 12:34, Rom 12:1-2,
Eph 4:30, Phil 4:8, Col 3:5, 1 Tim 5:22, Heb 13:4,
1 Pet 2:11, 1 John 1:7, 1 John 3:3

Pillar 4:
Purpose - Unlock What You Were Created to Do

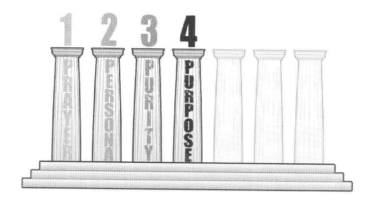

Don't be afraid to give up the good to go for the great.
- John D. Rockefeller

You can be marked by the past or make your mark in the future. The choice is yours!
- Anonymous

A few years back, the book "The Purpose Driven Life" by Rick Warren broke records as thousands of churches embraced the importance of teaching about purpose, and tens of millions of people bought the book. Warren's simple message was received with passion because the average Joe struggles to know if he is living his purpose.

It might be difficult, but knowing God's purpose for us is worth the struggle. When we know our purpose, we can handle disappointment without growing discouraged. We can hit homeruns when life throws us a curveball. We can protect our relationships from unnecessary conflict. We can do what we know is right even when our decisions seem crazy to other people. All of these benefits come from seeking and following God's purpose. Let's get started.

What is Our Purpose?

A *Legacy Minded Man* seeks out his purpose, looking for the specific reasons God put him here on earth at this time in history. Then, a *Legacy Minded Man* gets to work fulfilling that purpose.

Two Bible verses from the book of Jeremiah make five things clear about our purpose in life. As you read, picture God speaking these same things directly to you.

Before I formed you in the womb I knew you, before you were born I set you apart; I appointed you as a prophet to the nations. - Jeremiah 1:3

For I know the plans I have for you, declares the Lord,
plans to prosper you and not to harm you, plans to give
you hope and a future. - Jeremiah 29:11

God Made You and Formed You

Just as a sculptor shapes a lump of clay into something he can use, God actually shaped us and formed us, so that He could use us to accomplish His purpose. Similarly, God's plan in creating us resembles that of an engineer who designs something with a specific form and structure to meet a specific purpose. That's what God has done for each of us. Our existence is not a random event. God has shaped, molded and designed us for a purpose! We all go through times when we feel bad about ourselves. This verse reminds us powerfully that no one is an accident or a reject. God made us for a reason.

God Actually "Knew" Us, Before We Were Formed in the Womb

God is all knowing. He knows everything about us and has known everything about us since before the time of Creation. This gives us two choices. We can either ask Him to show us our purpose, or we can fumble through life, trying to figure things out for ourselves. Sometimes we are surprised by a weakness in our character. Or on the positive side, we discover a hidden talent and wonder how to use it. These things weren't in God's blind spot. He knew about them, good or bad, all along. And He's ready to use them as part of His purpose for you.

God "Has Set Us Apart" for a Purpose

Our culture, the media and our educational system try to drag us onto a manmade path through life, forcing us to just "go along to get along." The world's system tempts us because it's popular. But, at the end of the day, it's not the right thing for people set apart by God. One of the reasons so many men have mid-life crises is because, they bought a ticket to the system's path early on. When they get halfway to their destination, they suffer buyer's remorse. These men have spent their lives working toward the system's goals and dreams, only to end up disappointed. In an effort to regain lost time, true purpose, and meaning, they often throw away the first half of their lives, and hurt the people they have met along the way. Jeremiah reminds us that God's purpose for His people is different than the one the world promotes.

God Already Knows the Plans He has for Us

The question of purpose is not an unsolvable mystery. And we don't have to figure it out by ourselves! Some men look for their purpose like kids trying to hit a piñata at a birthday party. They are blindfolded, dizzy, and holding a stick, hoping their next swing will connect with their purpose and not one of their friends. God's way is different. He knows the purpose He has for you, and He wants to let you in on it. Our challenge is to walk with Him and talk with Him, learning His purpose as we go. We need to take off the blindfold (and put down that stick!).

God's Plans Are to Prosper Us – to Have Hope and a Future

People often think they can come up with a better plan for their lives than God! They act like they can out-create THE CREATOR and out-plan THE PLANNER. Others don't know or understand that God created them with a plan and purpose, so they just go with the flow, doing whatever seems right at the time. Still others, lacking a firm grasp on what God wants from their lives, are easily caught up in the schemes of others. Many of them get used or abused. These verses teach that God's plan for us is good, offering hope and a future. God's path is not a dead end street. As *Legacy Minded Men*, He already has the type of future that brings great hope and success planned for us!

Responding to Disappointment: "You Can't Always Get What You Want"

As men, we can get caught up in the lure of a dream or goal. When it doesn't work out, we get discouraged and forget to look for God's purpose. I experienced this about two years into my career. I was working with a headhunter to find a new job, and I interviewed at the Sealed Air Corporation.

Learning from my previous mistakes, I was both professional and polished. I left feeling confident that the job was mine. When I got home, the headhunter called and said, "I'm sorry Joe. They chose someone with a little more experience, but they really liked you and want you to come back to interview for a different position."

Believe it or not, that scenario repeated itself three times. All told, I interviewed four times at the Sealed Air Corporation. I never got the job. After the fourth interview, I was devastated. I bawled my eyes out.

The next day, a seemingly random wrong-number phone call put me in touch with another headhunter. She took advantage of her mistake to drum up business by asking if I was looking for a job. You betcha!

Through my new headhunter, I interviewed at another company and met the controller, Arnold Kezbom. Kezbom and I hit it off, and he hired me. I ended up following him to three jobs, each time getting a $5,000 raise. The whole experience gave me a well-rounded business background that provided the confidence I would need to eventually run my own business.

Before my success working with Kezbom, I had tried very hard to get a job at Sealed Air, and I suffered a great deal of pain when I was rejected there. But, God's purpose for me was different. He did not want me to work in the accounting department at Sealed Air. He wanted me to work at smaller companies where I could get experience and learn how to run a business and a ministry.

I didn't see the silver lining when Sealed Air turned me down over and over again. Most people don't when they are in the midst of a bad situation. I've learned to keep my eyes open a bit wider. You should, too.

Handling the Unexpected: Turning Curveballs into Homeruns

Things don't always go according to plan. Unfortunately, when situations veer away from the expected, we feel unprepared and uncomfortable. Knowing our purpose can take the sting out of those moments. When we know our purpose, we have a plan, and when we pursue our purpose, we get prepared for the plan. The unexpected becomes an opportunity. I learned a lot about this when life threw me a big, public curveball.

Sometime after I began the *Legacy Minded Men* ministry, I was invited to a Hispanic pastors' banquet in Jersey City. I didn't know a lot about the evening, but I wanted to be a part of honoring these men of God for their service. I had been busy, and I was tired. I looked forward to the event as a time to relax, have a nice meal and spend time with some men of God.

Imagine my surprise when I arrived at the banquet and saw my name listed in the program as the keynote speaker! At first I thought it was a mistake. It wasn't. With no advance notice, I would be called on to deliver the big message of the night.

I called my wife and asked her to pray.

This wasn't some pre-season game. I run a ministry for men, and the leaders I would address that night represented thousands of men. I clearly saw how my performance that evening could cause **Legacy Minded Men** to explode to the next level of influence or be a road block that could stop it in its tracks. No pressure!

I had no time to prepare a great message, so I had to trust in my persona, experiences, and, most importantly, God.

He delivered. In the moments before the event began, as I prayed fervently, God gave me the words to say – a "Divine Download." Despite the language differences and short notice, I was able to deliver a strong message in an uncomfortable situation. It was clear that God had a plan all along – to make connections that could impact Hispanic men in the days ahead.

He just didn't tell me all the details!

I realized something important that night. While I may not have had advance notice about the keynote speech, I wasn't totally unprepared. I had some history with God. I had spent years growing in my relationship with Him, and He had spent years preparing me for both expected and unexpected ministry moments. I had been soaking up Scripture for a long time, so that in the situation the Holy Spirit could pull it out of me, just at the right time.

It was a powerful night, one that I will never forget. I'm thankful for the unexpected opportunity, and I'm really glad that I was ready, because I had already discovered and pursued my purpose — to help engage, encourage and equip men to be who God created them to be.

My question to you is: "When life throws you a curve ball, will you have what it takes to stand in the box and hit it out of the park?"

Protecting Relationships: Focusing on What's Important, Even When Life is Rough

Knowing our purpose has the power to protect our relationships. This is especially true when the people we care about make mistakes that cost us time, money or effort. I learned a lot about this aspect of purpose a couple of years ago. It was a stressful time for our family. In August 2011, my home was flooded. We had about 10 feet of water in our home, and we were forced to move into a hotel for 99 days. Our vehicles still worked, and that was important because my son was learning to drive.

Flooding, relocation, driving lessons with a teenage boy – I was wound a little tight.

One day I took Jordan to an unfamiliar lot. He began well. But, when he attempted to park, he didn't notice the little brick divider at the front of the space. And, when he did, he accidentally hit the gas instead of the brake. The car jumped the curb.

When the car landed on the island, I screamed, "No!" and Jordan, more nervous now, stepped on the gas again, leaving the car teetering on the island with its wheels hanging off either side. None of the tires could touch the ground.

I asked Jordan to get out of the car, and I took over at the wheel. I gunned the engine, and the car flew off the island, but it was banged up. The back bumper had been pulled out, the exhaust system was about two feet longer than it should have been, and there were a lot of little things damaged.

In my mind, I was going insane. The car was brand new!

But, I also knew that how I handled the situation could hurt my son's confidence.

As I drove around a bit to see how bad the damage was, I prayed. "Lord, this has got to be a teaching experience. I don't want him to be afraid to drive because of my reaction. Lord, help me to respond well."

I calmed down and drove back to Jordan. I got out of the car, walked to the passenger side and told him to get in and continue to practice driving.

He said, "Dad, I'm really sorry."

I responded, "It's not your fault, don't worry about it."

Because I understood that my purpose as a dad at that particular moment was to instill confidence, I was able to use the moment to teach him, not scar him. The situation could have driven a wedge between Jordan and I, but instead, it solidified my purpose as a father. My purpose is to teach him and to be his biggest fan!

Sadly, as a parent, there have been too many times when I did not respond well. On this particular day, knowing my purpose helped me to do the right thing and get through a rough day with a significant relationship intact.

Bizlink

Sometimes knowing your purpose causes you to act in a manner that other people don't understand. Your purpose may lead you down a difficult road, and other people will think you are crazy for staying on the path. Remember, the opinions of other people aren't what matters most in your life. You were made by God for a purpose, and it's your responsibility to fulfill it, no matter how painful.

I got a taste of how hard fulfilling a purpose can be in 1998. I was the co-owner of a weekly newspaper with a mailed circulation of 70,000 pieces and $2 million in annual sales. Despite our success, my partner and I knew that the business climate was changing, and we decided to sell. The Internet and corresponding tech stocks were booming, and we took advantage of that opportunity, selling the paper for a stock deal worth about $1 million.

I thought it was a really nice deal, and it provided me the opportunity to start my dream business – a multi-media company called Bizlink. Bizlink was cutting edge and exciting. Investors thought so, too, and we effortlessly raised $1.3 million dollars for the start up. New York Yankee legend Don Mattingly became our spokesman and one of my partners. It was a thrilling time!

But, in April of 2000 things started to go wrong. The market crumbled, and there were internal problems at Bizlink. The company went bankrupt just six months later.

Two groups of people were hurt in the bankruptcy: employees and investors. I worked hard to find jobs for the employees. At one point I was offered a new job as a COO in a company. I thanked the person who offered me the spot, but asked him to use the salary he would have paid me to hire two of my former employees. He agreed and hired both men. All my former employees found work, but I was still unemployed.

I didn't have savings. And because the company that purchased my paper for a stock deal went belly up, I had nothing to show for the once valuable asset.

I wasn't the only one to lose out. As part of the corporate bankruptcy, roughly $250,000 in company debt would be written off. But, I knew the people who had loaned Bizlink the money, and I didn't want them to lose their investment. I just could not let that happen.

I talked with my wife, and we decided to take on the company's $250,000 debt personally. Our balance sheet looked like this: no job, a big mortgage, three kids, and a quarter of a million dollars in extra debt. Help me Jesus!

Some people urged us to declare personal bankruptcy, but we didn't think that was part of God's purpose for us, so we did not.

Enter Life and Leisure

The decision not to go bankrupt AND to take on $250,000 of debt put us under a great strain. It was an extremely hard time. I did a lot of jobs to earn income, but there was no clear solution or path forward. By God's supreme grace we made it through. To be honest, I have no idea how -- the numbers just didn't add up, but the bills got paid. It was a God thing.

In August of 2003, we decided to move away from New Jersey, to Georgia, where housing costs and taxes were much lower. Our reasoning was simple. We thought our home in New Jersey would sell for around a half a million dollars. With only half of that money, we could get a great house in Georgia and use the difference to pay off the $250,000 debt to our Bizlink investors.

Turns out that wasn't God's purpose for us either.

Shortly after we made the decision to move to Georgia, I was contacted by the owner of another paper, Life and Leisure. The man, whose name is George, told me he wanted me to help him start a new paper. I told him that I felt God was leading me to Georgia and he said, "No, no, you don't understand, God wasn't saying Georgia, He was saying 'George'., "I'm leading you to George."

George won me over, and we agreed to begin the new newspaper. Knowing the amount of work involved, I was reluctant, but I did not want to stand in the way of God's plan.

That willingness to follow God's purpose paid off. As we moved forward with Life and Leisure, God overcame obstacle after obstacle. At one point, we were required to pre-pay for our postage and printing, but we didn't have any money. A newly hired employee offered the money from a home equity loan she had just gotten. As everything lined up, I realized that God had His hand on this venture. Now, more than 10 years later, we are still publishing Life & Leisure. God has blessed that paper and my family through it.

There have been other times when I have had to choose to stick with God's purpose, despite other people's opinions of me. At one point, I was offered $350,000 for Life and Leisure. The money would have gotten us out of debt. But, the man who wanted to buy the paper told me that he would take all of the Christian information out of it. I opted not to sell.

I still remember the look on a good friend's face when I told him that I was going to turn the deal down. It was clear that he thought I was crazy.

I think God blessed that decision. A few years later, I sold 49 percent of the company for roughly the same amount I had turned down. I was able to pay off the majority of that debt that we had incurred from Bizlink and still have the company. It also provided the door to open to *Legacy Minded Men*.

The lesson is this: Fulfill your purpose, regardless of what other people think.

Just a thought...

The graveyard is the richest place on earth, because it is here that you will find all the hopes and dreams that were never fulfilled, the books that were never written, the songs that were never sung, the inventions that were never shared, the cures that were never discovered, all because someone was too afraid to take that first step, keep with the problem, or determined to carry out their dream.
— Les Brown

Have you ever sat down and really thought about your purpose? If God created you for a purpose – what is it? What are you doing to get there? Are you going to live out your dreams and purpose or bring it with you to the grave?

Pillar Builders...

- Write out a list of goals.
- Before I die, I will......
- In 10 years, 5 years, 1 year, I will....
- Within the next 30 days, ask someone to coach you in at least one area of your life to help you achieve your life's purpose.

One of the greatest things a man can do to achieve his purpose is to sit down with others who have already done what he is dreaming about doing. Ask those successful people what they think about your plans. Does your gift set fit your dream? In what areas will you need help? Do you have the right short- and long-term goals? Maybe they can coach you or recommend someone else who can. But remember this...there is no consultant more in tune with your purpose than the God who created that purpose in you!

Additional Study Verses...

Pro 19:21, Pro 20:5, Jer 1:3, Jer 29:11, Rom 8:28, Eph 2:10, Phil 1:6, 2 Tim 1:9

Pillar 5:
Priorities - To Live Out Your Purpose You Need a Plan of Attack

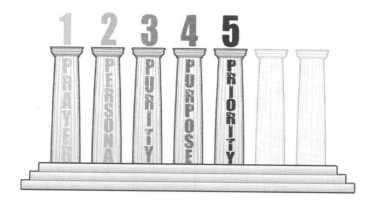

If you fail to plan, you plan to fail. – Harvey MacKay

"The Tyranny of the Urgent"

Life is busy. Incredibly busy! The days of working 9-5 and being able to retire at 55, with a nice pension to live on, may be gone forever. Endless things pull at us and beg for our attention. It's easy to have non-stop days and booked evenings. You would expect to have something to show for that much activity, right? But, when we look back at our busy days, we often struggle to identify any worthwhile accomplishments.

Culturally, we have more luxuries and less time, more social connections, but fewer real relationships. People have more access to us, which leaves less and less free time.

Economic forces drive many people to work harder than ever just to survive. Many of us aren't trying to keep up with the Joneses, we are simply trying to keep food on the table. At the other end of the financial spectrum, some people have more money and possessions than they could ever use, but they feel like their lives have no meaning.

Either way, we are challenged with navigating our schedules and making sure we are living the life that God created us to live. Unfortunately, there is always pressure from our culture to live to compromise or strive to live its definition of success. At some point, we can get sucked into lifestyles that don't bring God glory.

We've all had the experience of working really hard for something only to realize later that it wasn't worth the effort. Instead, it was a waste of time. Even worse, the goal was often achieved at the expense of something more important. We got sucked in, and we sacrificed our priorities for some type of busyness.

Charles E. Hummel, whose career included work as the faculty director of the Christian ministry InterVarsity Christian Fellowship, and served as the president of Barrington College, wrote a short booklet titled, "The Tyranny of the Urgent." In it he said, "We live in a constant tension between the urgent and the important." Urgent things scream for our attention, Hummel wrote, but truly important things — time for Bible study, prayer, reading good books, serving the poor -- don't.

The booklet was published in 1967. In it Hummel describes how telephones installed on the walls of homes robbed people of a quiet place, free from interruptions, where they could focus on and accomplish the important tasks God had for them. Imagine what Hummel would say about today's world where most people have access to the Internet, voicemail, text messages, Facebook, and Twitter, all in a pocket-sized device! Our technology makes the urgent more tyrannical than ever.

Learning to recognize important goals and stay focused on them, is an important part of becoming a *Legacy Minded Man.*

Priorities – The Tension of What We Need to Do and What Really Matters

You've got a mortgage to pay; you've got kids to feed. You're trying to make it all work. Why doesn't it? We have to manage the tension of the reality of these needs without neglecting what our heart is telling us is the most important.

The truth is most men already know what's important. Married guys would say it's important to spend time with their wives. Fathers would say that their children are important.

Many of these same men have not figured out how to establish a regular date night with their wives, or spend more than a few minutes a day in conversation with their children. Eventually, many wake up in a house with a discouraged spouse who feels neglected and a distant teenager or young adult. Neither of these is God's will or produces great legacy.

So, how do we close the gap between what we "feel and believe" is most important to us and the reality of how we spend our time? Here's a simple answer: Make a plan. Stick to the plan. The plan takes a big idea like "love my wife," and breaks it down into concrete actions to accomplish.

Thinking out concrete steps to accomplish our priorities is an area where most of us fail. We don't plan to focus on what really matters, with the result that our lives are consumed by too many non-essential things.

As adult men, we need to remember what it was like when we played football, basketball, or another sport. We had a plan. We had a playbook and memorized the plays; we had practices scheduled and went to them; we scheduled gym time and worked out. But when it comes to our real life and our priorities, we often don't win because we have no plan. It's not that we are not trying, it's that our energies are spent somewhere else. Then, when it comes to what matters most, we run out of time or have no more fuel in the tank!

Once we have a plan in place, we have to stick to it. When God wanted Moses and the people of Israel to remember the Ten Commandments, He carved them into stone. That's how we need to approach our plans for the important things in life. That date with your wife or talk with your kid can't be changed on a whim; keep it written in stone.

Legacy Minded Men learn to build a plan to succeed at what matters most in life. Setting non-negotiable priorities allows them to navigate a world of never ending demands.

Two events stand out in my mind when I think about living by a set of priorities. In the first, my clearly defined priorities and a serious commitment to stick to them, no matter the cost, kept me from hurting my little girl in a way that could have left lasting damage. In that situation, I knew what to do because I knew my priorities and I had a plan. Let's take a look at a time when I got it right.

A Father's Love

During the 1998 World Series, first baseman Tino Martinez swung his bat and changed the entire complexion of the contest between the New York Yankees and the San Diego Padres. Clearly, this was one of the most exciting games the Series has ever produced, and to have it occur in New York made it even bigger.

I have been a serious Yankee fan since I was about 10. Quite frankly, the Yankees were the first thing I ever really locked onto. During a difficult childhood in which I had no self-esteem or self-confidence, baseball became my release and the Yankees the object of my affection.

Years have passed, but my affection for the Bronx Bombers burns strong. I still receive a tremendous amount of pleasure watching the team play and following their progress. My passion for the Yanks has been strengthened by the opportunities I have had to get to know many of the players through Baseball Chapel. I also got close to the baseball scene through my first book, **"Safe at Home."**

Since I have been a fan, the Yankees have been involved in 12 World Series, including the magical season of 1998. I made a determination that year that the team was good enough to get to the Fall Classic, and I was going to make it a point to be there to cheer them on. To guarantee me a spot, I purchased a partial season ticket plan, which gave me two tickets for every Friday night game at the stadium. It also assured me of two seats for the first game of every playoff series, including the World Series. I attended the first two playoff series and had an incredible time.

However, just about the time it became apparent that the Yanks were headed to the World Series, my wife mentioned to me that our church was having a father-daughter dinner. "Great" I replied, "When is it?"

She replied, "Saturday, October 17th."

I immediately cringed, thinking that the date could also be the first game of the Series! The tickets did not have a date on them, so I called the Yankees, and they confirmed my fear: the first game was on the 17th. I then asked the ticket sale representative if I could trade the first game for the second game of the series. Their reply was simple: "No exchanges! No returns!"

I slumped. My dream of attending a World Series was now in serious jeopardy. What could I do? I called several ticket brokers and asked if they would be interested in trading the October 17 tickets for the following day, a Sunday. They were happy to buy my tickets, but they wanted me to pay two times as much to get a new set for Sunday. The price was too high: not an option!

The bottom line became very clear; if I wanted to go to the Series, I had to go on October 17.

I talked to the Lord about it, knowing already what the right thing to do was. My daughter Jenny, who was 6 at the time, then asked me in that incredible way of hers whether or not we were going to the dinner.

At the time she asked, I was reading the sports page. On the front of the paper, was a big story on the

Yankees with a picture of some of the players. After Jenny asked, I told her something very special was happening that night, and I held up the paper and pointed to the picture. Her bright smile faded. I could tell that she felt that I had chosen the game over her.

I couldn't stand the look of hurt on her face. Still pointing to the picture, I smiled and said, "It is a very, very special night because it is going to be OUR NIGHT!" Her smile returned even bigger than before. I don't know if she knew what I was giving up, but I am sure she knew exactly where she stood in my eyes. It is not something she will never forget, nor will I.

I will never forget it because five minutes after we got to the dinner, Jenny asked me if we could leave. I calmly got down on one knee, and looking into her eyes, told her that we would be staying for the length of the dinner! We did!

We arrived home just in time to see Tino hit that grand slam, and you know, it was ok that I wasn't there. After all, I got my money back for the tickets and, yes, made a little extra coin, but more importantly, my daughter knew that no game, or meeting, or ANYTHING will ever be more important than her!

Choosing Between a Good Thing and a Legacy Thing

We need to apply the test of priorities to ministry opportunities as well.

From 1995 to approximately 2008, my wife and I ran a charitable organization called Adopt a Child. We worked with the local Division of Youth and Family Services to help abused and neglected kids. Many of these kids had been removed from their homes or were being closely watched by counselors. We wanted to bless them, so we contacted DYFS to see if we could provide some gifts at Christmas time. The social workers agreed and provided us with names and Christmas wish lists.

We promoted Adopt a Child through the newspaper that we co-owned. Many people responded and gave faithfully for many years. We collected gifts at our house, so that they could be distributed in a confidential manner. One particular year, we had over 3,000 gifts in our home at one time!

The program was a success. Over the course of 12 years, we had over 20,000 children "adopted" and secured approximately 50,000 gifts for these kids.

For a couple of years, we included a copy of the Gospel of John with each present.

But sometime during 2007 and 2008, my wife and I began asking ourselves, "Is this really a benefit, giving a child a gift during Christmas?" Even with the Gospel distribution, we weren't seeing fruit. Eventually, we concluded that there was no lasting, eternal value in the program.

Even though people praised us, and we were on the front page of the daily newspaper twice, we just knew that it was not the most impactful thing we could do with our time and resources.

Ultimately, we had to prioritize where we were spending our time, and we decided to pull the plug on Adopt a Child, choosing instead to invest in something with more spiritual impact.

That decision led to the formation of *Legacy Minded Men*.

Sometimes the good can be the enemy of the great. In order to say yes to one thing we must say no to something else. At times like these, having established priorities is essential to help you think and plan clearly.

A Jar of Rocks and My Overly Hectic Life

A man who was teaching on priorities had a large jar and several large rocks. He placed five or six large rocks in the jar until no more could fit. Then asked his audience, "Is the jar full?" almost everyone shouted "yes!"

He smiled and pulled out a bag of smaller rocks and dumped them in until no more could fit. He said, "Raise your hand if you think it's full now." About half the hands went up.

He smiled again, pulled out a bag of sand and poured it into the jar until it couldn't hold anymore. Then he asked "is it full now?" Everyone was more skeptical and only a few hands went up. People were catching on.

Lastly, he pulled out a jug of water and poured water into the jar until it overflowed. He said, "Is it full now?" and everyone shouted, "Yes!"

He then paused and asked the question, "What was the point of this example?" The answers began to fly:

- You can always add a little more.

- You should never be satisfied with the amount of things you are doing.
- If you try harder, you can always do more!

The crowd was very pleased with itself until the speaker smiled one more time and said, "You are ALL wrong – VERY wrong".

He said, "The moral of this example is this – if you don't put the big rocks in first, you will never fit them in. You see, we often lose in the areas that matter most because our time and energy are spent on the little things that consume our time and energy and keep us from winning when it matters most."

Many people cringed as they realized this was a picture of their overscheduled, under-prioritized lives. Their lives were packed with the small rocks, the sand, and the water. "Their jars" were full, but they were not doing the things that mattered most.

Interestingly, you can skip your priorities and still seem "successful" to the outside world. But, every time I have done so, I have felt like a failure on the inside.

I've gotten it wrong many times, but when I gave up the World Series, I was able to take care of two important priorities. I built up my little girl and my wife because I put the big rock in the jar first. Yes, the Yankee game was important, but it paled in comparison to the grand slam smile on my daughter's face. I still enjoyed the home run and the win by television, but more importantly, I won as a father and a husband – priceless!

Similarly, when my wife and I gave up Adopt a Child, we were able to put the "big rocks" of sharing the gospel and helping men grow in their faith into the jar. If we had kept distributing gifts, we wouldn't have been able to accomplish what God had placed on our hearts as most important. These were both tough emotional decisions but I wouldn't go back and change either one!

Just a Thought...

What matters the most in your life – what really matters? Why don't you sit down and make a list of your priorities. Are you scheduling real and sufficient time on what matters most? Are changes needed? If so, work towards putting those changes into practice. If something matters to you, schedule time to get it done.

God made you to win. Having a written game plan will help you win! I (Jack) have benefitted greatly by first writing down priorities, and then scheduling my day in hour long chunks of time that are committed to the priorities I listed. It brings focus to what is most important on the job and in life.

Legacy Minded Men have clear priorities and a game plan to execute them.

Pillar Builders...

1) List your top 5 priorities.

Spending time with God
Church
Family
Work
Living Spring Water

2) Schedule time working on or doing those priorities – list time daily or weekly that is committed to your priorities.

3) In our busy schedules, we often have to say

"no" to something in order to say "yes" to something else. What are some things that you need to say "no" to so you have the time, energy and resources to say "yes" to your priorities?

Additional Study Verses...

Josh 1:6-9, 1 Chron. 28:19-20, Psa 1:1-3, Pro 24:27, Pro 27:23-27, Pro 29:18, Luke 14:28

Pillar 6:

Perseverance – Tough Times Introduce You to Yourself!

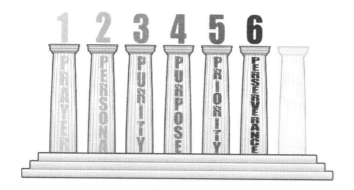

New level, new devil.
- Pastor John Orlando

Pain can be a great teacher.
- Joe Pellegrino

Rome wasn't built in a day, and a legacy that outlives you won't be built in a day either. A legacy that blesses your grandchildren and great-grandchildren will take a tremendous investment of your time, energy, and resources. As you seek to build a lasting legacy, you will face trials and temptations. You will be tempted not to persevere.

The Bible has a lot to say about how we should handle trials. Trials come in many forms:, crises, conflicts, or problems. At other times, simply the frustration and time it takes to get things done can be a trial. Whatever form your trials come in, if you don't know how to keep going, you can kiss any chance of building a lasting legacy goodbye! Let's look a little deeper at how the Bible says that we should handle trials and how to persevere through them.

Trials? Our Friend? Really?

Consider it pure joy, my brothers, whenever you face trials of many kinds, because you know that the testing of your faith develops perseverance. Perseverance must finish its work so that you may be mature and complete, not lacking anything.
- James 1:2-4

Count trials and hard times as joy? The scripture literally means to welcome trials as friends! Does that mean I should be glad that bad things happen? Yes and no.

James is not telling us to be a masochists whose idea of a happy life is getting a beat down! To understand a verse of scripture, you often have to keep reading for things to make sense. In verse four we see the result of counting our hard times as joy: we become "mature and complete, not lacking anything." Now that's what I'm talking about.

Trials help us develop perseverance, which plays an essential role in each of us becoming mature men. Without trials, you won't develop perseverance, and you won't become a mature man. Lasting legacies are built by mature men, not by men who give up every time they face a challenge.

For professional fighters every loss is a challenge. Yet there is usually one loss in particular that is a turning point in a fighter's career. The loss devastates them because they realize that they may have great skills, but they don't have the character or stamina to achieve their dreams. They realize that if they don't make SIGNIFICANT changes, they will never be anything more than an undercard fighter. They may never get a title shot! Some of these fighters need to switch coaches or camps; others have to get a new diet or new training partners. The bottom line is that fighters who want to win make a decision to make a permanent change.

Are you ready to make the decision to change? If you want to hand down a different legacy to your children than the one you received, you need to make the same type of commitment. You need to learn how to turn your trials and losing moments into game changers.

In general, people want the prize at the end of the race, but they don't want to run the race. Others run the race, but are not willing to put in the training that will qualify and prepare them to win. A *Legacy Minded Man* is focused on the end game, the win. He is willing to persevere through whatever life hands him because the prize is worth whatever it takes to get there!

A yearlong frustration and trial taught me a lasting lesson about perseverance.

The Fourth Time

I love baseball. There isn't a better sight than a freshly cut ball field on a warm spring afternoon, and no sound hits the eardrum like the pop of a glove or the crack of a bat. I can trace my love for the game all the way back to when I was ten years old, and my father took me to my first Yankee game. I haven't looked back since!

Ever since, my life has been filled with collecting baseball cards, memorizing statistics, playing games until college and now watching games. Some might call it an obsession, but to me it is a simple passion. There is just something magnificent about this sport we call America's Pastime.

You might gather from this that I am a rather passionate person. I'm the kind of guy that falls deeply in love with the things I appreciate.

Besides my family, there is only one thing that I am more passionate about than baseball, and that is my Lord and Savior Jesus Christ. It took some time for me to understand my need for salvation and to take on this passion towards my faith, but once I did, it became my ever-burning fuel.

When I became a Christian, I tried to marry my passion for baseball and my passion for Jesus by writing a book about Christian baseball players. As outlandish as that idea may have sounded to those who didn't share my passions, it made perfect sense to me.

Before I began my research for the book, I had a "Field of Dreams" mentality -- "If you build it they will come." I assumed that Christian players would bang down my door to be interviewed for my book. No such luck.

Fortunately for me, one of my business associates was a former New York Yankees baseball player. He was able to wrangle me the "Holy Grail" of Major League Baseball: the Major League Baseball Media Guide. The book contained highly confidential information about where players stayed when travelling, and it was all mine. I was in my glory!

As I devoured this book, I came across a listing for something called Baseball Chapel. Instantly intrigued, I looked into the listing to find that it was the perfect marriage between my passions for faith and baseball. I found that Baseball Chapel was an organization that commissioned chaplains to conduct short chapels for Major League Baseball teams and to disciple players who sought discipleship. My knees weakened. As I read on further, I nearly collapsed. The headquarters for this fount of Christian-baseball goodness was only fifteen minutes from my house! Fumbling for the telephone, I quickly dialed the number that was listed and put in a call to the Executive Director Dave Swanson (the same Dave Swanson I mentioned earlier).

The voice that answered the phone said, "Dave Swanson here." I spilled out my own introduction, and then said, "Mr. Swanson, I love the Lord and I love baseball. I am looking to write a book on Christian baseball players, and I was hoping that you could put me in touch with some of them." I was greeted with silence on the other end.

Then he said, "Why don't you go ahead and call me in three months to discuss further."

Despite the eternity that three months would be, I agreed to his request and waited three months before I called him again. When the calendar finally advanced to the date circled in red with the words "CALL DAVE SWANSON" written on it, I dialed him again.

Much to my surprise he said, "Call me in another three months."

Once again, I agreed and marked the date on my calendar. After three more months elapsed, I called him again. To my utter dismay, he told me again to call him in three months.

I was confused and more than a little annoyed, but no length of time would stop me from getting the information I sought. If this was the man who had what I needed, I was sure going to play by his rules.

Three months later, a full year after my first phone call to Swanson, I looked at the calendar, which indicated it was time to call and receive yet another three month sentence. Or was it?

"Yes, Mr. Swanson. This is Joe Pellegrino, you asked me to call you back in three months regarding helping me with my book."

His response, "Meet me at the Kin-Lon Diner in twenty minutes."

I'm not sure if I actually hung the phone up. Darting up the stairs and into the bedroom, I quickly changed from my dirty gym clothes into a pressed shirt and a tie. Within minutes of the invitation, I was on my way to the diner. When I arrived twenty minutes later, I found a tall, imposing, bald man waiting for me at the entrance. I said "Mr. Swanson?" He nodded.

I stuck out my hand out and instead of a handshake, I received a piece of paper. He then turned toward the dining room to find a place for us to sit. As I stared at him in amazement, I glanced down at the piece of paper in my hand. On it were the names of Major League Baseball players whom he considered to be strong Christian men. I couldn't believe it.

Before he could find a seat, I touched his shoulder, "Mr. Swanson. Forgive me, but why now? Why after a year?"

"Take a seat Joe", he said as he directed me to a booth.

As we sat, I was perked up and ready to listen. Swanson smiled. "My family used to own the Thomas English Muffin Company. At one time, I was in charge of purchasing. Whenever a salesman called, I never bought from him the first time. If he came back a second time, I still did not buy from him. Nor did I do so if he came back a third time." Mr. Swanson's eyes were glued on mine. "But if the salesman persisted enough to return a fourth time, then he had a customer for life. You just did that."

What a lesson in perseverance I learned that day. So many times we give up or grow discouraged when someone says "not now" over and over again. In many cases we grow discouraged by even one "no" response. In his first letter to the Corinthians, Paul writes:

Do you not know that in a race all the runners run, but only one gets the prize? Run in such a way as to get the prize. - 1 Corinthians 9:24

You know that in a race all the runners run, but only one wins the prize, don't you? If we are to get the prize, we have to run like we mean business. Giving up at small obstacles will get us nowhere, but if we persevere, keep our eyes on the goal, and keep running, we can experience that elusive place where success and purpose become one.

Unfortunately many times we give up just when we should persevere a little bit longer. Paul writes in Galatians, "Let us not become weary in doing good, for at the proper time we will reap a harvest if we do not give up." (Galatians 6:9)

While some of God's promises are unconditional, many of them give a clear condition that we have to meet. This verse has a condition. It's like a contract. If one or both of the parties does not meet their side of the contract, the agreement is nullified. We know that God never breaks His side of the deal, so we're the deal breakers.

Our side of the deal in this verse is to "not give up." We will reap a harvest at the proper time, but God tells us not to give up! Many people are mad at God when something that they hope will happen doesn't. But they are the ones who didn't follow through with their side of the bargain. They broke the deal and are mad at God, really?

Hardship is a part of life. We can wish it were otherwise, but the reality is that we all will face trials. Paul writes in 2 Tim 2:3, *"Endure hardship with us like a good soldier of Christ Jesus. No one serving as a soldier gets involved in civilian affairs —he wants to please his commanding officer."* To leave a legacy, you must endure hardship.

Paul uses the metaphor of the Christian as a soldier who is single minded in his purpose and does not allow himself to get "entangled" with civilian matters. He is wholly focused on his mission and the battle at hand. *Legacy Minded Men* need that same single-minded focus so that they are able to persevere during hardship.

Other places in the Bible, such as Ephesians 6, make it clear that as Christians, we are in a spiritual war. One of the reasons the devil comes after men so hard is because if he can wipe out or ruin a man, he is able to wipe out or ruin an entire legacy, possibly for generations! The many problems and challenges fatherless boys face show what happens when men don't leave a legacy.

Being a **Legacy Minded Man** is not a game. It's not cute. It's not just dressing up and going to church to please your wife. We have an enemy who *"prowls around like a roaring lion looking to devour us."* (I Peter 5:8) We need to be on our guard. We need to endure hardship like a good soldier and never forget Who we serve. The race of life is not won by the fastest or the one who looks the best, but by the one who perseveres and builds each and every day.

Just a Thought...

On a scale of 1 – 10, 1 being an absolute quitter and 10 being "I'll die before I quit!" – Who are you? Who are you when life throws everything at you including the kitchen sink?

What are your biggest regrets? Which ones could you and should you go back and fix or do differently? Regret is an ugly thing. Today is a new day for you to do a new thing. This time, commit to sticking it out!

Pillar Builders...

- What is your most important long term goal that you will commit to NEVER quitting on?

- What is an area where you feel like quitting but know you shouldn't?

- In what area of your life do you want purity, but compromise when stressed out?

- Who do you have in your life to encourage you or kick you in the pants when you need to keep going?

- If you don't have that person, what is your plan to get someone like that in your life?

Additional Study Verses...

Rom 5:3, Gal 6:9, Eph 6:18, Phil 3:14, 2 Tim 2:3-4, 2 Tim 3:10, Jam 1:2-4, 2 Pet 1:6

Pillar 7:
Power - Holy Spirit Unleashed, He will Provide Opportunities You Never Had Before

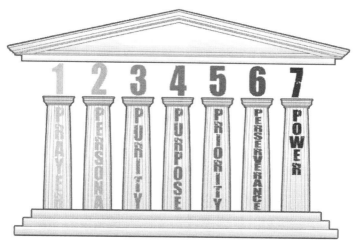

The cross exists because we have failed.
- Anonymous

God opens doors...but it is your job to walk through them.
- Joe Pellegrino

When you are born again, God gives you the Holy Spirit to literally come and live inside of you. This is the same Holy Spirit that raised Jesus Christ from the dead and now raises you from being spiritually dead to spiritually alive. And it is the same Holy Spirit that gives you the power you need to follow Jesus each and every day of your life. 1 Corinthians 4:20 says, *"For the kingdom of God is not a matter of talk but of power."* This is a man's scripture if there ever was one! Let's take a closer look at what this means.

First we have to realize that God is a King, and He rules His Kingdom. In God's Kingdom, He is in charge. He has dominion. What He says goes. When we choose to follow Jesus, we leave our little kingdom where we tried unsuccessfully to control everything, and we enter into His Kingdom.

Limited or Unlimited Strength – Which do you Choose?

When we rely on our own strength, we become limited by our weakness. But God is omnipotent. That means He is all-powerful. Choosing to follow Jesus means giving up control of our lives and relying upon Jesus to be the power source in our DAILY lives. We need to stop using our own limited strength and abilities to follow Jesus and choose to follow Him in our thoughts, actions, and decisions. We have access to HIS unlimited power through the Holy Spirit. Let's use it!

The Same Power That Raised Jesus from the Dead

When we choose to follow Jesus, the Holy Spirit literally comes and dwells and lives in us. This is this same Holy Spirit that raised Jesus Christ from the dead! Romans 8:11 says, *"And if the Spirit of him who raised Jesus from the dead is living in you, he who raised Christ from the dead will also give life to your mortal bodies because of his Spirit who lives in you."* This goes way beyond a guy who is dragged to church by his wife on Sunday morning. It's about the raw power of God living in us and working through us! There is something in men that loves power. We jump when we see a crushing home run, a monster dunk, or a knockout punch. We are wired for power! Following Christ is not about going to church and passively listening and forgetting what we heard. When we go to church, we go because we want to learn how to walk in the power of the Almighty God! Christ doesn't want to modify our behavior. He wants to revolutionize our lives!

The Purpose of Power

God gives us power to achieve His purposes! Those purposes include building strong marriages, conquering sinful habits in our lives, and being great fathers for our kids. What would your life look like if you functioned in more of God's power and less in your limitations? For far too long, men have spent their lives living in the power of the flesh instead of the power of the Holy Spirit!

The Generator

I mentioned that in 2011 our house flooded. In 2012, Hurricane Sandy hit, and we faced the threat of even more flooding. However, something almost worse than flooding happened, the power went out for seven solid days! How do you survive with no electricity for an entire week? Fortunately, we were blessed to have a generator. Unfortunately, when I tried to start the generator, it wouldn't start. I kept trying, but it just wouldn't turn over. I went through all the connections and they all seemed good. Since we had never actually used the generator before, I thought I might be overlooking something. I asked a neighbor who is mechanically inclined to take a look. He flipped the switch, pulled the cord, and it started right up. I was dumbfounded. I asked him what happened and he said, "You never engaged it. You had the fuse set to off." Many times, when we want to plug into power, we fail to engage; we fail to connect in a way that turns the power on!

I had a generator capable of powering my house, but it was not functioning. Similarly, many men have faith in Jesus as their Savior, but His strength is not running their lives. The connection is not being made with the Holy Spirit. Sin or unbelief is short-circuiting their connection to the power of the Holy Spirit. They are not allowing the Holy Spirit to direct and empower every aspect of their lives, which means no power. My problem was not in the generator, but in the connection.

There is a great difference between calling Jesus our savior and calling Him our Lord. A Lord controls you, you yield to his wishes and hand him the keys to your life. This is a tough thing for men to do, but if we could fully understand the power that this generates, watch out!

Breaking the Chains

One of the reasons we work so hard at *Legacy Minded Men* is because so many men are held in the chains of sin. Some men don't care because they love their sin, at least for a season. But at some point, many men realize that the very thing that they would have called freedom and fun has sunk its teeth into them. The very thing that they once bragged about and enjoyed now owns them. Over time they begin to hate it. Often, they don't know how to get out of its grip.

So many men, including good family men and

even surprisingly many church leaders, including pastors, have become entangled in ongoing sin such as pornography. Others are in the chains of alcohol, drugs and all kinds of sexual sins. Some are looking for the next thrill, many others use their sin to medicate themselves from the pain of life.

When you come to Christ, the Holy Spirit gives you the power to break these sins. Just think if the Holy Spirit was powerful enough to raise Jesus from the dead after three days, then He is powerful enough to break ANY habit or sin you have. *Legacy Minded Men* has an ongoing ministry called "Breaking the Chains." This is a conference phone call where men can call in and hear from other men who have experienced the power of the Holy Spirit breaking patterns of sin and sexual addictions in their lives. Many of these men struggled for years and some even for decades, but thanks to the power of the Holy Spirit they found freedom.

Pretty Good at Drinking Beer

Not only is "Pretty Good at Drinking Beer" a country song, but for too many men, it is also their favorite hobby. It sure was mine, and I was sure good at it! I (Jack) began drinking on a regular basis when I was a freshman in high school. My friends and I got our start sneaking liquor from our parents' liquor cabinets. We would hide it in shampoo bottles and drink it on the boardwalk at the Jersey Shore. Then we started drinking beer and just kept on going.

Unlike many, I was a successful drunk. I managed to complete high school, earn an academic scholarship for college, and after my undergraduate degree, go on to Columbia University where I completed three master's degrees in two years. I could close the bar three or four nights a week, and still get up for an 8:00 AM class the next day. It was a gift! It also allowed me to live a lie, and perpetuate a VERY self-destructive lifestyle. Along the way, I hurt a lot of people and left a highway of relational wreckage behind me.

One Sunday morning in the summer of 1997, I heard a preacher tell the story of Jesus and how He came to pay for my sins so that I could be forgiven. He said that I could actually know God and that He would give me a new beginning. This was the first time I had ever heard this good news. Church people call it the gospel. I wasn't interested in a bunch of religious stuff or joining a church, but I did want a new beginning. I needed to be forgiven for a whole lot, and I did want to know God.

I asked Jesus to forgive me and to come into my heart. I asked Him to give me the strength to follow Him. I meant it, but I didn't really know what I had done. In that moment, I opened up my heart, and the Holy Spirit came and dwelt in me. I began a new life. Church people call it being "born again". I was not only forgiven, I was instantly set free. From that moment on, I have never had another drink. From my understanding, when you have been a heavy drinker for ten to twelve years, stopping overnight is impossible. But that's what happened to me. In a moment, the Holy Spirit made me a new person. He is able to do the same for you. He brought life to my dead soul.

You Can't Handle the Truth!

OK – yes it's an old movie line, but we love it! It highlights an important truth for us as Christians: we can't handle all the truth at once. Jack Nicholson actually stole the line from Jesus!

In John 16:12-13, God says, *"I still have many things to say to you, but you cannot bear them now. However, when He, the Spirit of truth, has come, He will guide you into all truth."*

Jesus was telling his followers that He still had many things to tell them and teach them, but they were not ready. There have been times when I know that either God or people are telling me the truth about things, but I either don't know how to make the changes or just don't want to (yet). But the Holy Spirit living within us keeps working on us until we are ready. We can reject the truth and in turn reject God's power. However, that's not God's will for us, and it is a surefire recipe for a lousy legacy! God is patient with us, but we can definitely speed up the changes and release His power into our lives by allowing God to guide us.

We leave many things on the table when it comes to God. We need to stop doing that. Our kids, our wives, and the world need us to be walking in His power!

The 364 Day Old Check

Back in 1989 when I left my job to start my own business, it was lean times. It was very difficult as we tried to make a business work. I didn't know that much about starting a business, even though I had learned how to run a business. It was an interesting time and like I said, it was lean!

During this time I was really struggling to pay my mortgage each month. In order to make the little money we had go further, I decided to refinance my mortgage. In this process we had a month where we had no money and didn't have a clue how we were going to pay the mortgage. One day I received a call from my attorney. He told me that he needed the deed to my house. I had no idea where it might be, so I asked him where I would find it. He said that it would probably be with other papers from my last closing which I had done the previous year.

I keep all my important papers in the family safe. I unlocked the safe and began searching through the papers. I found an unopened letter from the attorney who handled my last closing. I opened the letter and sure enough there was the deed. I also started thumbing through the other papers in the envelope, and I came across something that was very interesting. There was an un-cashed refund check for almost the exact amount of my mortgage payment. I couldn't believe what I was seeing. I looked on the check and it was dated 364 days prior. One thing I had learned from my time in business was that banks will not cash a check that is more than 365 days old.

So I ran, I mean ran, to the bank! I went to the drive thru to deposit the check and the entire time, I prayed "Lord, let them say 'Have a good day'." Sure enough the young lady came back and said, "Have a nice day"! The check went through, and I was able to make my mortgage payment. I spent a lot of time praying and trying to understand how God was going to help me pay my mortgage. Then out of nowhere,

God leads me to a check that I received 364 days earlier. The check had been waiting in the safe for almost a year. All I had to do was open up the safe and cash the check in order to have what I needed. Are you tapping into the power of the Holy Spirit to provide the power you need to live a legacy minded life?

Just a Thought...

How would your life look different if you were walking in God's power in greater ways? What is stopping you? Have you settled for being a Sunday morning Christian who doesn't read the Word, speak it, or live it? In what areas of your life do you need to wave the white flag, surrender to Jesus and ask for His power?

Get a coach – nobody goes to the Olympics without a great coach. If those are physical races, how much more important is a spiritual coach. Yes, this can be your Senior Pastor, but who do you have in your life on a regular, even daily basis if needed, to coach you, encourage you and help you walk in God's power?

Pillar Builders...

1) Read and Study God's Word - Know the truth – the best way you can know the truth is to know God's Word.

2) Have a Daily Quiet Time – this is probably the MOST important thing you can do
   a. Pray
   b. Read God's Word

c. Focus on areas where you need growth – there are many great books and resources to help you grow. These can also point you to specific scriptures to focus on and live by.

3) Focus on growing and not just trying to stop behaviors. The Holy Spirit empowers you when you walk in obedience to the Word and His leading. The more time you spend with God and following His leading, the more you will walk in His power!

Additional Study Verses...

Psa 62:11, Zech 4:6, Matt 6:13, Mark 5:30, Luke 24:49, John 14:26, John 16:12-13, Acts 1:8, Rom 8:11, Rom 10:9, 1 Cor 2:4, 1 Cor 4:20

Epilogue - Now What?

Process – hey, maybe this is the next pillar? Just like salvation is the start line, not the finish line, your choice to become a *Legacy Minded Man* is NOT the finish line. It's the beginning of an amazing spiritual journey!

You became who you are today because of a process. That process is called "life," and you are where you are because of the life process you have lived.

This is NOT some type of New Year's Resolution!!!

Becoming a *Legacy Minded Man* is NOT like the average New Year's resolution that lasts a week or two at best. It's not simply a decision to be forgiven by God. It's also a decision to become a God-powered man whose life is something that can be proudly passed on to his children – both natural and spiritual.

One final illustration: When my son Joey was around 8, I would take him in the backyard and teach him how to play baseball. The deal was that if he hit the ball over my head, I would buy him a big Pirate

Lego ship. He really wanted that. Unfortunately, he never hit it over my head. Or did he?

My son thought he did. I disagreed. Regardless, it obviously bothered him because he thought that I reneged on the deal. As of this writing Joey is 24 years old. I finally recognized that the Lego ship was creating a wedge between us, and I decided that it was time I did something about it.

So when he came home for Christmas in 2013, I had a special gift for him. I asked him to read the card first. It said simply:

> *Joey,*
>
> *This is long overdue, and for that*
> *I am sorry. Please accept this,*
> *late as it may be, for the*
> *continual home runs you are*
> *hitting in your life.*
>
> *- Love Dad*

The look on his face told the story.

Gentlemen, no matter how bad you screw up, no matter how many years have passed, you can always do something about your mistakes. Even if the person you go back to fails to forgive you, you will be released. I am so thankful that I tried to right a wrong, and I believe that Joey and I are better for it! It's never too late!

If you want to be a *Legacy Minded Man*, it all begins with the right foundation. Jesus is the "rock," the only real, solid foundation that stays dependable no matter what! Once we have that settled in our hearts and minds, we can start building on the things we learned from *The 7 Pillars of a Legacy Minded Man*.

A *Legacy Minded Man* is more concerned with becoming something, than he is about checking off a to-do list. He is focused on understanding, not just some intellectual exercise. A *Legacy Minded Man* lives in two places at the same time. He gets up each day and fights to win the battle in front of him. He also gazes into the future and lives in a manner to build lasting legacy.

God created you to WIN! Always remember that you are not in this alone! God is on your side and so is an army of *Legacy Minded Men*!

Jesus is the foundation, God's grace is the cement and the Holy Spirit is the builder within those who rest in Christ's peace. Now that is a team I want to be a part of, how about you?

Congratulations on making it to the end of this book. Job well done! You have the game plan, you know about the *7 **Pillars*** that need your focus. You have asked yourself the tough questions; you have begun to create a game plan. Now get out there and win!

Additional Resources

Legacy Minded Men

www.legacymindedmen.org - is the site to connect for upcoming conferences, discipleship tools, small groups and much more. You can also keep up with Legacy Minded Men on Facebook and Twitter @LMMNJ

Mentoring 2 Manhood

www.mentoring2manhood.com – is a powerful resource for men, where men help men. This site is an extension of this book and provides an excellent source for men to grow!

Fourth Generation Ministries

www.4thgen.org - is a great resource for leadership training, regional conferences, youth ministry, blogs, books, podcasts and more with Jack Redmond.

Not Just an Average Joe

www.notjustanaveragejoe.com - is Joe's marketing website.